MA
H

You rock as a
"Trading Spaces Yk"
designer. Hopefully these
Books will give you some
ideas for future projects.
You _are_ Paige Davis !!! Have
a Great Trip Home. Happy,
Happy, Happy Birthday.
~ Leigh Ann

ANNE McKEVITT'S
designer know how

Published by BBC Worldwide Ltd,
80 Wood Lane, London W12 OTT

First published 2000

ISBN 0 563 55164 X

All photographs in this book, except for pages 12, 14, 16, 19, 21
and 22, are of the interior design work of Anne McKevitt.

Photographs © Anne McKevitt 2000, taken by Colin Poole

Commissioning Editor: Nicky Copeland
Project Editor: Khadija Manjlai
Art Director: Lisa Pettibone
Designer: Liz Lewis
Photography, Art Direction and Styling: Anne McKevitt
Set in Minion and Bell Gothic Light
Printed and bound in Great Britain by Butler & Tanner Ltd,
Frome and London
Colour origination by Radstock Reproductions Ltd,
Midsomer Norton
Jacket printed by Lawrence Allen Ltd, Weston-super-Mare

To Don, Baggy and Sooty for being there
when I needed them and making
themselves scarce when I didn't…

Colin Poole, whose photography, as ever,
made it all look marvellous…

And Annabelle Grundy, who without doubt
made my life bliss by transforming the text
on each project.

ANNE McKEVITT'S
designer know how

contents

design basics

Have you ever wished for a 'dream home'? It might combine the space of a loft, with the intimate atmosphere of a cottage. You might long for a hi-tech kitchen that's still cosy, or perhaps a minimalist Japanese-style bedroom, but with beguilingly seductive overtones, or even a twenty-first-century bathroom, all chrome, stone and glass, yet somehow still relaxing and luxurious under foot.

The chances are that you would like all these things and a bit more – a place to rest, entertain, work, think and, most of all, to enjoy. You will want to be able to adapt it to every mood and requirement in your life. As your needs change, you will probably expect your home to accommodate them. Circumstances might call for a home office today, a nursery tomorrow and an *en suite* bathroom some time in the future. You are going to demand a lot from your home.

Unless your idea of perfection is a huge manor house or a Bermudan beach-side apartment, you can go a long way to achieving what you crave without having to inherit a fortune first. You are going to need lots of discipline, effort and some expert knowledge to guide you through both the subtleties of design, and the nuts and bolts of getting the job done. Armed with these things, there is really nothing to stop you.

it's your life

Whether you are embarking on refurbishing a whole house or just one room, the first step is exactly the same. Be absolutely clear in your own mind about what you want to achieve. Whatever you do, don't start with colours, fabrics or the look you want to create – this will all come later. It is paramount at the beginning to concentrate on making your space work for you.

The best place to start is with yourself and your lifestyle. Imagine you are planning a complete overhaul of a sitting room. Ask some simple questions: What do I want to do in this room? Will I entertain friends, play music, sew or practise yoga? What seating, lighting, storage and power points will I need? You must answer these questions totally honestly.

This might seem odd, but you are going to have to live with your choices every day. No matter how much you might lust after a minimally furnished, clutter-free room, it is just not going to work if you have hundreds of CDs and subscribe to eight magazines a month. Likewise, it is completely absurd to spend time and effort sanding and polishing floorboards if you love to sprawl on a carpet with the Sunday papers. If your way of life is at odds with your tastes, you will be much better off adjusting the look. Changing your decor is far easier than

Below: Natural shapes need not dictate a traditional look but can be interpreted successfully in a contemporary way.

changing your behaviour. Besides, you must be able to relax utterly in your own home. This will be impossible if it feels like someone else's, no matter how stunning it looks.

PLAN OF ACTION

Whether you are faced with a boring bathroom, poky kitchen or a living room you just can't live with, planning is crucial to the success of any change you want to make. You must be a hundred per cent disciplined because every decision, from the choice of flooring to the style of the door-handles, should be made before you buy a single item.

Likewise, you must work out the layout and position of each piece of furniture, power point, radiator and lamp before committing yourself to so much as a pot of paint.

As you look around your room, imagining how you would like it to be, the undertaking can seem daunting. Take courage because, as with many challenges, if you break it down into smaller tasks, each one will become manageable. Do yourself a favour and allow plenty of time. Never be hustled into a purchase or decision because of a discount, or pressure from a particular workman. There will always be another sale, and you will always find another plumber. It is your home and your money, so you are the one who should be in control, and you are the boss.

PICTURE THIS

Before you go any further, you need to be certain about what you are dealing with. It can be hard to visualize a room other than how it is at present, but if you are planning wholesale change, you must be able to see with total clarity the basic space you have. This can be especially awkward in a bathroom or kitchen where there might be fixed items which you plan to throw out, or which have to be incorporated

into your design. You might also be thinking of knocking down a wall between two smaller rooms to make one big space, and the result can be very difficult to envisage.

The most foolproof place to begin is with an outline, to scale, of the area you are going to work on. It is imperative that this is drawn absolutely accurately because you will rely on it as you experiment with layouts and calculate which items of furniture can be accommodated in each location. And if the thought of graph paper and rulers sends you into a panic, contact an architect, who will be able to convert your room to a flat plan. Some professional input is well worth the relatively small fee you will have to pay for it.

A cheaper alternative would be to find a newly qualified design graduate who could help you. Approach a local college and track down the department head concerned with interior design, structural engineering or architecture courses. He or she should be able to suggest recent graduates with the necessary skills, and you will probably find that college-leavers are only too eager for work and real experience.

However, if you are happy to draw this flat plan yourself, measure the area and sketch it on to a sheet of graph paper, marking the positions of doors, windows and other fixtures such as radiators or a chimney breast. Metric measurements are simple to use, and a scale of 10cm to 1m is convenient. Whether you prefer metric or imperial (1in to 1ft), stick to one system throughout or you could become totally confused.

Once you have completed the outline, ink it in. Then you can either photocopy your diagram several times, or use masking tape to stick a sheet of tracing paper over the top, on to which you can start to pencil in your layout. Peel it off and add a fresh layer for each variation you try. Another option is to cut out paper shapes to scale, representing the oven, bath, table or towel-rail, and move them around on the plan. This is especially relevant if you are working out a kitchen or bathroom design with several sizeable components to fit in.

3-D IMAGE

The next stage is to take your flat plan into three dimensions. A bit of imagination is required for this step because you are now going to visualize yourself actually living day to day in your new room. Mark the proposed positions of your furniture and appliances on the floor with masking tape. Don't forget that they will take up vertical space as well, so, where feasible, mark heights on the walls, too. It's very easy to overlook obstacles such as wall-lights or a ventilation fan, but this way you will avoid any mistakes. Make sure a chest of drawers or kitchen unit positioned under a window does not come up higher than the sill, and be aware that a cupboard sited in a corner at right-angles to a window or light source will seriously reduce the amount of light coming in from that point.

You might not have the luxury of a completely empty room to mark out. You might have to imagine how the new plan will operate once old units are removed, or a wall has come down. Again, give yourself plenty of time to think things through, and use the space you can delineate in conjunction with your flat diagram.

GOING THROUGH THE MOTIONS

Your plan is an invaluable part of the design process, but it's just a representation of a changeable, three-dimensional room which surrounds you. There's only one method of checking how your ideas are going to work in practice, and that's to pace out the daily tasks you will perform in the room. In a bedroom, for example, picture yourself opening the wardrobe. Which side should the door be hinged? Is there enough space to open drawers without hitting the bed? In the bathroom, can you reach a towel easily from the shower? When you are relaxing on the sofa, is the phone to hand, or will you be leaping up whenever it rings? Spend some time on this exercise to make quite certain that everything combines comfortably. After putting in time, effort and expense, you will be more than disappointed if you notice awkward little problems that could have been ironed out with more forethought. If you feel a bit foolish acting out your bedtime routine, or preparing a pretend breakfast, you might prefer to do it in private, but it's well worth a bit of embarrassment if it avoids future frustration.

MEASURE UP

A sizeable chunk of your budget should be put aside for furniture but, as with designing and decorating your home, there's more to choosing your pieces than simply falling in love with a plush purple armchair or basing your entire kitchen around a scarlet range cooker. The thought process is just the same as that applied to your space. The first question has to be: 'What do I want this item of furniture to do?' If you are considering a bookcase, for example, you will need to confirm that the height, depth and width are compatible with the spot you have chosen for it. On top of that, you must ensure that the shelves can hold the books or folders you want. Miss out this vital check, and you will feel totally exasperated with yourself, when, too late of course, you realize you will have to store tall volumes or files on their sides, which looks messy. There are few things more irritating than badly used space, particularly when it is in short supply to begin with, so make life easy and do your homework before you hand over your money.

Measure the insides of cupboards and wardrobes as thoroughly as the outsides. This could involve two shopping trips instead of one – first to measure in detail, then to purchase – but it is time well spent, and there is no other option to avoid an expensive mistake. Think about the clothes you will be storing in a wardrobe. How much full-length space should there be for coats and dresses? You can hang nearly twice as many shirts, skirts or trousers in the same area in two layers, but confirm the length of the longest garments before you commit. Will there be enough room for shoes and boots, and what about bags, belts and ties? Could you utilize the top of the wardrobe, say for storage boxes, or will it just disintegrate into a chaotic mess? You know yourself better than anyone, so make the right choice for your own peace of mind.

Even a cosmetic touch can go awry if you don't check sizes properly. You might have a rug in mind, a colourful splash on the floor to set off your polished boards to perfection, only to find that the boards are all but concealed because the rug turns out to be larger than you remembered. Similarly, assess the height, depth and width of lamps, especially if they are to sit on a wall-mounted shelf. With hi-fi equipment, don't forget to allow space for moving parts to lift up or outwards. Study the space that each object is going into, and picture it functioning in position, taking into account what you are planning to put next to, above or below it.

get the idea

You have only to walk into your local newsagent's shop to see the plethora of interior design magazines available today. Having flicked through many of them, including some imported from Europe and the USA, you might feel that they are the best source of inspiration when you are planning your home, and you will indeed find some pointers here.

SPACE-SAVING DOORS

These are one aspect that can be adjusted successfully in a restricted space, so keep in mind the following possibilities if you find yourself in a tight corner.

- For a small kitchen or bathroom, consider a sliding door, which takes up next to no space. There are plenty of good-looking choices around.
- Re-hang doors to open against a wall, rather than into the main area of a room.
- If a hall or landing is big enough, hinge a door to open towards you rather than forwards into the room.
- Convert a bathroom door into a pair of smaller ones to save space. (Due to fire regulations, this idea might not be suitable for a kitchen.)

Below: A semi-translucent glass door extends an invitation to explore what lies beyond.

However, if you want to make something truly unique and personal for your home, you have to look behind these 'set pieces' and uncover the roots of an idea. You can be your own designer, originating an individual style, rather than picking up on someone else's thoughts. To do this, you need to absorb stimuli from absolutely anywhere and everywhere.

Suggestions could come from the shape of some furniture you spot in a café, the colour of a dress or a nail varnish, the outline of a building in a photograph, or the surface of a piece of sculpture. A film or TV programme might reveal an exotic location or historical period that could be your starting-point. Many of the best designs exist in nature and you won't go far wrong observing the organic forms and colour combinations you find outdoors. Tones and textures of bark, flowers, pebbles or whole landscapes can all fire your imagination. Studying finished rooms is undoubtedly relevant, but it is the decoration and materials in them that produce the overall result, and these could stem from virtually anything.

HEAPS AND HOARDS

Keeping this in mind, start recording and gathering together pictures and examples of everything that appeals, whether it's a beach scene, some glassware, or the way a cabinet is constructed. Carry a small camera wherever you go and photograph that unusual door-handle, nifty folding chair or glorious skyline. Tear pictures out of fashion, nature, style and other magazines. Pick up clothes, jewellery and trimmings, postcards and other objects that strike a chord with you. Don't go anywhere without a notebook to jot down addresses and phone numbers

Left: The beauty of this bathroom is its simplicity, from the style of the fittings down to the choice of plain towels and toiletries.

of sources, as well as thoughts that occur as you are looking around. When you are stuck in a traffic jam, or waiting at a bus stop, you will be amazed just how many useful phone numbers you will start spotting on the sides of vans, so keep your eyes open.

Begin to amass your samples and images well in advance of when you want to get going. If you collect over, say, a year, you will be able to track how your tastes change and see when what was an object of desire becomes a cliché. This will help to confirm your choices, as well as showing what you can live without. It's also useful to keep a few examples of styles or items that you detest. They will clarify your requirements when it comes to instructing, say, a carpenter or curtain-maker.

As with any project concerning your home, all the above steps must be sensibly organized if they are to be of any value to you. Label a separate box file for each room, into which you put all samples, cuttings, photos or notes relating to it. There might be components, such as flooring or a paint-shade, that you are planning to use in more than one room. Keep the reference in one box but write yourself a reminder and put it in the other box. With all the information most of us carry in our heads these days it is very easy to forget, even if you are convinced you will not.

FILTERING THROUGH

When the time comes, put the entire contents of, for instance, your living room box on the floor and study it. Start sifting through, setting aside anything that you no longer like. Then try to group similar ideas together. This might take a while. There could be items in the box that you have picked without quite knowing why, but the reasons will be revealed as you examine them. For example, you might have stored away a postcard of a wonderful aquamarine ocean, a cutting of a fantastic turquoise sofa and a rich peacock-blue silk scarf. It looks as if this colour family is a favourite that you would be comfortable using in your home. As you sort the collection, you will see a pattern emerging, which will help you to identify the style, colours, textures and overall character you will be happy with. The whole exercise should also clear your mind of any other possibilities that might have been floating around, so you can concentrate on translating your plans into reality.

TAKING SHAPE

The next step is to compile a mood-board. This is simply a notice-board, or large piece of card, on to which you stick all your chosen fabrics, paint samples, wallpapers, flooring and tiles, and pictures of furniture, lighting, vases and photo frames, even a shower curtain if you have found the one you like. You might have seen mood-boards in interiors magazines or design shops which might well have resembled works of art, but don't let this put you off. It really doesn't matter if yours is less than perfect. It's a working tool, not an ornament, and you must be able to move pieces around to use it effectively.

A mood-board is a really useful device for a designer. It gathers all the separate components of a scheme into one place to check that they all work together. It can also highlight factors that are missing, or indicate whether there is too much of one colour or texture. You might adore the honey-coloured wood flooring, the caramel velvet upholstery fabric and matt butterscotch paintwork as single elements, but as a group they could seem lifeless. A mood-board will allow you to experiment with some contrasting shades or accessories to offset each item and bring the whole concept together. It is also portable, so if you are working in an area with a fixed feature, such as a fireplace or fitted carpet, the mood-board can be positioned next to it to judge the effect. It's vital to keep your mood-board in the room to which it applies for at least a few days. Check it at various times to make sure you like what you see in the morning, afternoon and evening. Dark navy, for example, might look very dramatic in daylight, but it can become almost black in the evening and be overwhelming.

As you accumulate samples of the products you are considering, always ask for more than you will actually need. For example, if you are thinking of using two paint shades, get samples of at least six. When you see them alongside the rest of your selection, your second choice might fit in better than your favourite. You will save time and frustration if you label everything clearly. Record relevant information such as colour names, reference numbers, measurements and also where you found each item. You will kick yourself if you cannot remember where you spotted the perfect light fitting or that heavenly fabric. Also attach a note of prices, as this is essential when it comes to budgeting.

When you are finally happy with every single component on the mood-board, the golden rule is to stick to it. If you find yourself drifting away from the original choices, or unable to make up your mind, there is something amiss and you need to go back and reconsider your plan. Remember, at this stage you should not have parted with a penny, or committed yourself to any purchases, so take your time.

mind your money

It is an inescapable fact that, whatever alterations you want to make to your home, you are going to need some money to achieve them. It's not only sensible, but crucial to your whole project that you

Above: Modern and rustic styles combine with the mix of steel and wood components.

wholeheartedly take on board this important aspect, planning your finances with the same care and attention that you lavish on your furnishings. If you overlook a proper budget, you could at best end up with an unfinished room, and at worst dangerous fittings and huge debts.

Decide first how much you can afford to set aside for, say, refurbishing your bedroom. It is best to save a lump sum to get the major work done in one hit so that your room is not out of action for weeks on end. If you have a weekly or monthly income, you could then decide to allocate a regular amount to purchase the finishing touches in stages. Be totally honest and don't promise yourself you will give up buying clothes for three months if you know deep down you won't be able to do this. If you overstretch yourself, you will be storing up some serious trouble, so be rational and realistic.

FINANCIAL FUNDAMENTALS

Having worked out what you are happy to spend, there are two rules to observe. First, whatever sum you have arrived at, stick to it. If you have thought through everything sensibly, your figure will be reasonable, so there should be no excuses for overspending. However, if you see an item you truly desire, it can be excruciatingly difficult not to splurge. Don't panic, but think of ways around it. Can you put down a deposit to secure the piece and save up the balance? Consider approaching your bank for a loan, but, as ever, be completely straight about what you can afford to pay back each month. If you are really torn, ask yourself which is worse – owning or not owning it – and then decide.

The second rule is to spend only about three-quarters of the budget in your plans. This might sound silly but no matter how well you prepare, something unforeseen always crops up. It might be a minor irritation, such as a small price rise on a certain component, or a major headache, such as discovering that your home needs rewiring or a new damp-course. You cannot ignore problems such as these if they come to light, and you will be helpless if you have no funds to fall back on. It is also highly probable, especially if this is the first time you have tackled a design project, that a few things will be forgotten. No one, not even the professionals, remembers everything every time, but don't be caught out – keep some money aside as a safety net. If you have some cash left over once the venture is completed, give yourself a pat on the back and start planning the next one.

HARD SELL

Are you anticipating a trip to the sales, thinking this is the best way to make your budget stretch that little bit further? If so, think again. There is no doubt that there are bargains to be snapped up at sales, but there is skill to successful sale shopping, without which you could be heading for a costly calamity. The secret is to buy only basic items, which will not age or date. Look for plain towels and bedding, pillows or cushion-pads. Consider cookware, pans and electrical items. Steer well clear of anything patterned, or 'of the moment'. Shops have sales primarily to shift unwanted stocks, not

as a favour to their customers, and you will soon learn to spot the rejected items masquerading as irresistible offers.

Whatever time of year you are shopping for your home, be purposeful. Don't drift around the stores looking at anything that catches your eye because you will achieve nothing. Before you set off, have in mind what you are going to buy and resist the temptation to wander off course and browse. Take your notebook with you, containing all measurements, samples and other relevant information. If you do find an amazing object that you fall in love with, and you can afford it, don't necessarily deny yourself. The personality of a home evolves through a unique combination of selected pieces, so don't be too rigid.

TAKE IT BACK

No matter how carefully you shop, expect at least one purchase to come to grief. Objects can be faulty or you just might not like them when you get them home. Safeguard yourself by keeping every receipt. Put these into your purse or wallet as soon as you get them, and never into a carrier bag from which they tend to disappear. When you get home, jot on the back what they relate to, as this is not always clear and you might forget. Remember, three months or longer could go by before your cushion starts to fray, or a crack appears in the wardrobe door. It is also sensible to keep all the packaging, too, for at least a month, just in case you need to return the goods.

Don't forget guarantees. Fill these in and post them off straight away, attaching the receipt to the part that you keep so you will know exactly when and where the item was bought. Get organized with a couple of plastic wallets, one for receipts, the other for guarantees. Make a habit of always putting these important bits of paper safely away as soon as you can. This way, you will always know where to lay your hands on them.

Above: Enormous sofas, monumental plants and a large, decorative
fireplace highlight the grand scale of this living room.

MONEY MONITOR

Receipts are also a vital part of budgeting, helping
you to keep track of what has been spent. Once work
starts, you might need to review your budget as
often as every other day, especially in the early stages
when you are laying out money for materials. In any
event, you should update your sums at least once

a week to avoid overspending. If things are starting
to go wildly off course, take action immediately.
Revise your time-scale to give yourself a chance to
save up and prioritize tasks. When your room or
house is finally complete, it can be enlightening to
compare what you have actually spent with your
initial plan. Try to figure out why events went the
way they did. There will be lessons to be learned
from whatever happened so that you don't fall into
the same trap twice.

HARD CASH

Before you buy a single thing, set out your budget on paper so that you know where the money is going. Make a list of every item you want to purchase and how much it costs.

Measure floorspace and walls to estimate the quantities of carpet, tiles, paint or wallpaper you will need. Remember you might have to apply at least two coats of paint. If you are doing the work yourself, you will need the proper tools, so check out the prices of paintbrushes and rollers, trays, dustsheets, primer and so forth. Nowadays, there are water-based paints – far kinder to the environment than oil-based products – which are suitable for walls and woodwork. If you buy these, look out for synthetic bristle brushes. You will find these give the best finish with water-based paints. Also look into hire costs for larger tools, such as floor sanders. All these extras have to come out of your original sum, not your safety net, so do your research well in advance so you know what to expect.

GIVE AND TAKE

If you keep a chunk of money aside, you will be able to adopt a flexible approach to your plans. Some items might have gone up a little, so you need to decide whether you should still buy them or look for alternatives. Other ideas might prove to be too pricey when you get down to the details. If this happens, try to reach a compromise. For example, covering the whole bathroom with hand-painted tiles could come to a lot more than you had imagined, so what about using them on just one wall and offsetting them with a less expensive plain tile on the other three walls? If the entire project seems to be getting out of control, try to identify the key pieces that are integral to the look and then reconsider your secondary choices. This way you can cut costs considerably, but still maintain the essence of the design.

sourcing

Whatever you have in mind, you would probably like to make a trip to a large shopping centre, visiting household names to see a comprehensive selection of fabrics, lighting, furniture or crockery. Major stores are an obvious place to check out, and in many you might be pleasantly surprised at the ranges and ideas on offer.

However, not everyone has access to the high street. If you live in a remote area, have transport difficulties, or simply lack the time or inclination for shopping expeditions, you might think you are condemned to a dull home with dated décor and no spark of originality. Nothing could be further from the truth.

ARMCHAIR SHOPPER

A great many companies today, from the familiar retail giants to small specialists and craftspeople, have catalogues and a mail order service. A large number also have websites you can shop from, so no matter where you live, most products should be available to you. Shopping by phone and post is on the increase and will continue to grow in importance as lifestyles become more pressurized and we seek results ever more quickly. The Internet and TV home shopping open up yet further possibilities.

Begin to build up catalogues as early as you can, alongside pictures of products torn from magazines (see Heaps and Hoards, page 12). Sources are usually listed at the back. If something appeals, send or phone for brochures straight away, rather than waiting until you are ready to place your order. Use different coloured sticky notes for each site – kitchen, bedroom, etc. – to mark the pages showing products that interest you. In this way, you will not waste time leafing through catalogues and magazines to locate that chic little soap-dish, clever collapsible clothes airer, or perfect paint shade. Try not to rip pages out of a catalogue unless it is very bulky and not easily portable.

DEVILISH DETAILS

Of course, buying something mail order is never going to be the same as having the chance to hold, study or operate it before you hand over the money, but there are common-sense procedures you should go through to minimize the risk of disappointment when you open the packaging. Pay close attention to every point in the description. Check the dimensions given and try to visualize what the product will be like from the details of the materials used. For example, a blond wood bookcase might look very attractive in a photograph, but the little word 'veneer' in the description forewarns you not to expect a solid wood construction. Photographs do not allow you to experience textures either, so glean as much as you can from descriptions of fabrics and trimmings. Price can also give a fair indication of quality. Remember to check that delivery to your door is included in the cost.

SAMPLE SERVICE

In many instances samples can be sent before you confirm a purchase. This is commonplace for textiles, such as curtain fabric or carpet, but is also generally available for tiles, flooring, wallpapers, handles, worktops and many other components. It is often simply a question of asking for them. If you are firm, few companies will refuse and risk losing a potential sale. Nevertheless, they might expect you to order curtain fabric or wallpaper from a sample the size of a postage stamp, so request a full square metre. This is especially important if you are considering a large-pattern design. There may be a charge for this, but it will be cheaper than blindly ordering something that you do not like or recognize when it finally arrives.

If it proves impossible to obtain a sample, consider carefully whether to proceed with the purchase. To a great extent, this will depend on what the item is, how much it is costing and how important it is to your overall scheme. If you do go ahead, agree in writing with the company the terms and arrangements for returning articles, should you need to. Check that the sender's insurance covers anything damaged in transit in either direction.

Despite all your efforts, there will be occasions when goods have to go back for any number of reasons. Some companies make this harder than others, but in all instances, pack the item really carefully to ensure it does not get damaged, check insurance in case of a breakage or loss and include all relevant paperwork.

the team of experts

There is a saying, 'If you want something done properly, do it yourself,' and many people would opt for such self-reliance if only they had the confidence and the skills. There are many aspects of home renovation that you can tackle independently with the help of a DIY manual and some perseverance, and you will probably experience a huge feeling of satisfaction when the job's successfully completed. Nevertheless, you will undoubtedly need to call in the experts at various stages, so it is helpful to be armed with some hints on how to find the best professionals.

Think of yourself as the project manager. You will be employing and overseeing skilled workers and ensuring that the results are what you want. Start by setting up a job file. Put in dividers to create sections for the different tradespeople you will be using, such as builder, carpenter or plasterer, and file all relevant paperwork such as quotations, plans, contact numbers, references and receipts for goods and labour.

LOCAL LAW

Decide what skilled people you need to bring on board. As well as the obvious ones, such as an electrician or plumber, you might need to find an architect or structural engineer. If you want to knock down a wall, or alter the roof or exterior of the building, it is essential to consult a structural engineer, and an architect can take a great deal of the pain out of planning a substantial renovation.

If planning permission is required, such people can also smooth communications with your local council. The idea of dealing with the planning office might bring you out in a sweat, but there is no cause for concern. Planning authorities are not there to obstruct you, but to save you from making costly mistakes. Without their approval of your plans, you might be in breach of building or conservation regulations and could face a fine, not to mention unnecessary grief.

Above: A blend of textures and fuss-free furniture produces a tranquil bedroom with a Scandinavian flavour.

Depending on the complexity of any queries that arise, you can either contact the planning department yourself – and save a bit of money on your architect's fee – or ask your architect to deal with the matter. If it is a complex problem, it is advisable to leave it in experienced hands as there will be lengthy forms to fill in, and permission could be needlessly refused if inaccurate responses are given. In any event, it is absolutely essential to consult the planning department about major works, and you might well be lucky enough to hear that no special permission is required.

DESPERATELY SEEKING

When you are looking for any skilled worker, whether it is an upholsterer, decorator or glazier, the

QUOTES AND ESTIMATES

Unless you are very experienced and have time to spare, there will be certain aspects of the job that you will have to pay someone to do for you.

- Most plumbing and building work is best tackled by an expert, unless you know exactly what you are doing, and a qualified electrician is essential.
- For each task, get at least three quotations from recommended tradespeople. Insist on a quotation, not an estimate, as there is a world of difference. A proper written quotation should itemize all materials and labour charges and is a legally binding agreement. An estimate is more like a 'guesstimate' – guesswork – and final costs could be far in excess of the initial figure.
- Be warned: an unscrupulous firm could take advantage of a trusting client and give an estimate that turns out to be something less than half of the eventual price. Do not settle for anything but a firm quotation with which you can budget accurately.
- Make certain that there are no loopholes in your quotation. Think the job through and check that absolutely everything is included. For instance, a builder might quote for removing your kitchen and fitting a new one, but fail to mention disposing of the old units. To avoid paying extra, check details such as these.
- Does the builder's quotation include paying for skips? They are expensive and he might expect you to pay, which could be a hefty bill if you need several. You might also have to apply for a permit from your local authority.
- If you do get into a dispute, refer back to the quotation. If, for example, you have failed to specify that the electrician's quote must include making good after wiring your lights, you cannot expect this to be done without a charge, so take responsibility yourself for preventing costly loose ends.
- Take on board the fact that your workmen will ask for some money before they begin in order to buy materials (see Up Front, page 21).

safest way is to ask around your family, friends, colleagues and neighbours. Although personal recommendations from someone you trust are never a hundred per cent water-tight, they are the best guarantee you are likely to get. If you draw a blank here, then you will have to fall back on the columns of *Yellow Pages* or local newspapers. Anybody advertising through local newspapers or cards in shops is clearly seeking work but, more importantly, they are not generating enough jobs through word of mouth, and you should bear this in mind. The most sought-after tradespeople hardly ever need to advertise, as their clients' contacts become their next customers. This does not mean that anyone you find through an advert will be unsatisfactory – everybody has to start somewhere – but you should tread carefully and be aware of the pitfalls.

SPOT CHECK

When you find a likely firm, there are a few indicators you can look out for that will tell you a great deal more about the operation than will the workers themselves. There are clear signs as to whether a builder, for instance, takes pride in his work and reputation, and respects his clients. On the initial visit, is he on time and does he look presentable? You can't expect a suit and tie, but neither should you be subjected to dirty overalls and muddy boots. Does his vehicle look clean and in reasonable condition? Can he give you home or office addresses and phone numbers you can check out? Never accept a mobile phone number as the sole point of contact as you just cannot verify that person's background. Under no circumstances should you ever consider 'bargain' offers from passing labourers who appear uninvited on your doorstep offering to fix your chimney, roof or drive for a cash payment. Such people are con men, whose only skill is in helping their victims to part with their money.

Before you commit yourself to employing any skilled tradesperson, you will, of course, ask them to quote for the work (see Quotes and Estimates, page 20). It might seem cynical advice, but you should bear in mind that tradespeople can assess you and your financial position by the location and style of your house and the car outside, and might raise or reduce their charges accordingly. If necessary, park the Ferrari up the road while they take a look, and never give any hint of how much you might or might not be willing to spend. Ensure you get a total price for the complete undertaking, never a daily or hourly rate. Listen and take note of what each expert says as they inspect the proposed job, but remember that they might try to talk you into non-essential extra work, so question everything. You are in charge and you should tell them what you want from them, not the other way around.

To get any sort of comparison, you need to obtain three quotations for the work. There might be quite a difference among them, so you must analyse each one and note what is included or excluded. If anything is the slightest bit ambiguous, phone and get it clarified. As and when you decide to go ahead, it is wise to confirm in writing every item and task covered in the quotation, especially anything agreed verbally. You do not want to find out later that the price for knocking through a new entrance did not include fitting the new frame and door.

UP FRONT

Your workmen are almost certain to ask for some money before they begin in order to buy materials. This is a perfectly reasonable request, so don't be fazed, but do be prudent. Whatever you give them, particularly if it is cash, get them to sign a receipt. It is of no consequence if they think you are over-cautious or even a little odd. You need to be absolutely sure all the time about how much money

SAFE AS HOUSES

Having accepted a quotation and arranged a starting date, you should consider a few points before you actually let anyone into your home. Remember, you do not know these people well, so even though they are probably totally trustworthy, don't take any risks. There could be a team of at least two or three workers there at any one time and it only takes one rogue to cause an unpleasant upset. So just be sensibly security-conscious, particularly if you are away all day while the work is being done.

- Don't flaunt expensive hi-fi equipment, TVs, videos or cameras. Conceal as much as possible.
- Don't leave cash, jewellery, credit cards or other valuables lying about.
- Restrict access to rooms, unless connected with the work, and do not give any excuse for wandering around your home. Direct workers to a downstairs toilet, if possible, rather than sending them upstairs.
- Consider leaving personal papers and financial documents etc., temporarily with a trusted friend or relative, or with your bank.

Below: Rather than playing up original features, a plaster-and-paint finish can bring the modern look of a loft to a barn conversion.

has gone out, and where to. It is easier in the long run for everyone if the facts are spelt out on paper so there is no opportunity for a dispute to arise.

As the project progresses, you could find yourself dissatisfied with the standard of workmanship, timekeeping, cleanliness or a host of other aspects. In this situation, remind yourself once again that you are in charge and are paying people to carry out the agreed tasks. Point out firmly whatever is not up to scratch and insist on mistakes being corrected. If matters do not improve, you should seriously consider sacking the team before they do further

Below: A row of three simple windows brings light to an otherwise dark corner and also punctuates a blank expanse of wall.

damage. The least painful way is to request a figure for what you owe to date and write out a cheque. As you hand it over explain politely but firmly that you are unhappy with their work and that the arrangement is at an end.

CASH OR CHEQUE?

When the job is completed, a contractor might offer to waive VAT if you pay cash. This can be a tempting suggestion, as you would save yourself a significant sum if you agreed, but it is not advisable. If you settle in cash, you are unlikely to get a receipt, and without a receipt you have no comeback if a problem occurs later. If you have not paid your VAT, it would be very hard to pursue any future claim effectively. The more straightforward and above-board you keep matters, the fewer loopholes there will be if something goes wrong.

Hold back the final instalment for as long as you need to check that everything is functioning properly, and never pay in full until the very last touches have been done. Otherwise, you could wait weeks for someone to drop by and fix the handles on your kitchen cupboards, or touch up that last bit of paintwork. Your trusted team will have moved on to the next job and it will be virtually impossible to get them back.

time well spent

A home is unique and personal to its occupant(s). There are probably bits you love and bits you loathe. Everyone wants to live in pleasant surroundings, whether it entails major rebuilding or simply rearranging furniture. Whatever is involved, enjoy the process as well as the results of the changes to your home. Revel in the new skills you will pick up – maybe tiling a wall, shopping in cyberspace or negotiating with a tricky builder. Relish the sense of achievement and, above all, make time to savour it fully.

REFERENCE PREFERENCE

If you are satisfied so far with your tradespeople's attitudes and quotations, ask for names of previous clients and contact them. A bona fide contractor will have no problem with this, and you will have a golden opportunity to find out exactly how past work progressed. A less-than-honest contractor will give you the names of friends primed to make the right noises, so be on your guard. Inspect at least three commissions, and ask lots of questions, including:

- Was the client happy with the standard of workmanship? Make a really detailed examination and form your own opinion.
- Did the work start and finish on time?
- Was the quotation accurate, barring any unforeseen problems?
- Were the labourers careful and courteous?
- Was the site left tidy each night, and well cleaned at the end?
- Would the clients use this firm again, or recommend it to their best friends?

It does not follow that the most expensive quotation will result in the highest standard of work, nor that the cheapest will be the poorest. Consider the quotations in tandem with your judgement of previous work and overall impressions, then make your choice.

Above: Take advantage of an office-at-home situation and introduce some fun into your decor.

livingspaces

Would you like your living room to stand out from the crowd? There is a formula to the look and arrangement of our living spaces which it is all too easy to adopt without realizing it. Does your rug sit squarely in front of the fireplace, just like your neighbours' rug? Do you have a coffee-table flanked by a sofa and two matching chairs, just like those of your best friends? Do the same two or three colours appear on your curtains, flooring, upholstery and walls? It is time to break the mould.

More than any other room in the home, the living room can fall victim to 'sets' of objects. The obvious culprit is the three-piece suite – and in the same category come co-ordinating curtains, cushions, lampshades, tiebacks and tablecloths. Mix-and-match wallpapers with teaming stripes, patterns and borders are another example. If you are not too confident and would rather let the shops show you what should go into a design, furnishing a room in this way can be a sort of safety-net. The results can be attractive, but rather predictable, and you will miss out on any spark of originality.

If you are really nervous about your ability to make the right choices, a mood-board (see page 13) will definitely help. This is a vital tool for an interior designer. Without having to commit to a single purchase, you will be able to get a clear idea of how each fabric and component will look both in the room and alongside all the other elements. Visualize a board for a room with co-ordinating soft furnishings, a matching carpet, lamps and tables all in the same finish. Looks a bit boring? Too much of the same style? Just by changing one or two aspects you can start to inject some life and individuality into a scheme. The most interesting homes are those that have evolved over time, where the owners have accumulated favourite pieces rather than buying a complete set off the shelf.

When you buy items for a room, make sure that you keep all the receipts in a safe place; then, if you are really unhappy with something when you see it *in situ*, you can easily return it.

fresh start

Whether you are starting from scratch or revisiting a set-up you have grown used to, the planning strategy is the same. Step away from all your preconceptions and look at the skeleton of your room. Forget what has gone before. The sofa does not necessarily have to stay opposite the fireplace, and it is possible to reposition a TV point. Just changing the layout of the furniture can make an enormous difference – opening up a room, increasing light and revitalizing existing objects. Of course, certain fixtures, such as windows or a chimney breast, will have to remain, and you might not be changing everything in the room from the carpet upwards, so take account of what will need to be incorporated into the new design. Within a living room, there are elements such as wallpaper, a rug or lamp that you will be happy to replace after five or so years, but you might want to keep a sofa or coffee-table for ten years or longer. Bear this in mind when you are planning how much to spend on each item.

PLUG IT

Plan your room on paper, with a scale drawing (see Picture This, page 9) and think through how you want to use the space. List all the functions you want the area to perform and the equipment that needs to be accommodated. Decide on the positions for your phone, stereo and television, and plan the socket points for each at the appropriate heights. If you are having wiring work done to install power points, don't skimp. Put in a few extras, rather than risk resorting to adaptors and trailing flexes, which are dangerous and messy. Don't forget you will need to plug in a vacuum-cleaner, and possibly an iron and power tools.

TV HEAVEN

The location of a television is an important consideration. It needs to be at the right level for watching comfortably and, if possible, with its back to the main source of daylight. If it is opposite a window, you will not be able to see the screen clearly as there will always be a reflection on it. Your TV might be your pride and joy, a multi-media digital extravaganza, in which case you will want it to be a prominent feature. Alternatively, you might feel that when it is switched off, it should not dominate the room. Hiding it inside a cabinet is a good solution when you want to encourage conversation.

LIGHT TOUCH

Natural light is one of the best features of many homes and you should maximize whatever there is in a living room. It is far more pleasant to while away an afternoon with the Sunday papers if you do not need to switch on lights. Windows framed with heavy swags and voluminous drapes have given way to the neater treatments of roller or Venetian blinds, or fine, loose voile. Heavier curtains might be needed if your windows are draughty, but you can opt for a contemporary fabric, such as a fine wool, fake suede or sheeny velvet. Use less fabric than usual for a sleeker finish.

FUNDS FOR FLOORS

Carpet, especially if you like to sprawl on the floor to read, is the most obvious choice of flooring for your living room, but polished floorboards or laminate flooring with rugs can also work well. Carpet, however, gives the most comfort and warmth under foot.

Expect to spend a sizeable chunk of your budget, even if you go for an inexpensive choice. We often think of a carpet as a once-in-a-lifetime investment, and stretch ourselves to buy the best-quality,

CARPET CODE

- Don't spend a fortune. You might move house, or want a different carpet within five years.
- Don't waste money on high-quality underlays, unless you are definitely staying put for at least ten years.
- If an area is going to get a lot of traffic, choose the shortest pile you can, and look for a velvety finish. This kind of carpet will stand up best to heavy wear and will look good for much longer. A long pile will be very quickly flattened by feet and your new carpet will start to look old.
- A stain-resistant treatment is worth while, but as it is vital to deal with stains and spillage immediately, also keep some carpet cleaner in your home. If you leave a mark for any length of time, it will be all the harder to remove.
- If furniture makes indentations in your carpet, melt an ice cube on the spot and brush up the pile with a comb.
- Scrape up pet hairs carefully with a hacksaw blade.

Below: A carpet can bring together the style of a room by using similar colours and shapes in its pattern.

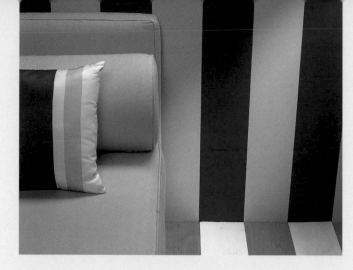

Above: Use one design element, such as a stripe, in different scales and tones to create a harmonious scheme within a room.

longest-lasting option we can afford. But a carpet does not have to be for life. Think of it more as a fashion item: go for a colour that appeals at a price you will not feel obliged to justify for the next twenty years. Underlay can add a hefty amount to the bill, so remember there is little point in buying the most luxurious one on offer if you are not planning to stay in the house for more than five years.

PERFECT SURFACE

You will probably call in a professional to lay your carpet, but there are certain preparations that are well worth making to ensure the best results. Don't lay carpets directly on to floorboards or underlay. If you do, you will eventually start to see ridges from uneven boards and grimy marks around the edges caused by draughts blowing dirt up from below the floor and through the carpet. First you must cover the area with sheets of hardboard. This is an inexpensive material that will ensure a completely smooth base for the underlay. The hardboard should be laid with the shiny side down on to the boards, and tacked into position every 30 cm (12 in) or so. Then you will need to fill any gaps around the edges with newspaper, and seal the perimeter with masking tape or carpet tape to stop any draught marks appearing. Be sure that the tape is completely flush with the floor, otherwise you will see it on the skirting board above the carpet.

sit the test

Furniture is a big outlay for the living room, but do not automatically assume that a sofa and two armchairs is the ideal combination. Two sofas will give you the same amount of seating, and can look neater and certainly more stylish. When you are trying furniture out in a store, do give it a proper test. What seems comfy for two minutes might feel too squashy, or too upright after ten or fifteen. Don't feel embarrassed – spend as long as you want sitting on a sofa in a shop. It is crucial to make the right decision because you will spend a lot of time, as well as money, on your sofa.

A sofabed can be a sensible purchase if you need to accommodate guests, but they are not ideal as the main sofa because the bed mechanism affects the springiness. Make sure that you are happy with the seating comfort before you worry about the sleeping facility.

COVERING NOTE

The choice of patterns, textures and colours for sofas and chairs is staggering, so it is a good idea to eliminate certain impractical types before you even start looking. For example, in a home with children, marks and 'accidents' are inevitable, so do not torture yourself by choosing plain, light-coloured upholstery, no matter how stylish it looks. For a family situation, a small pattern, such as a check or fancy-textured weave, will work best as stains and general wear and tear will not be so noticeable. Surprisingly, a large, bold pattern does not seem to disguise dirty marks as well as a small-scale one, and can look grubby quite quickly. Washable loose covers can help your furniture look good for longer. They will also allow you to choose a fabric or colour, such as plain white or cream, which you would not be able to contemplate for fitted upholstery.

Check out the work of your loose-cover maker before you agree on anything, and consider paying for extra touches, such as piping on seams, which will prevent the covers stretching and give a smarter finish.

ALL THE RAGE

Clothing trends can have a knock-on effect on furnishings: when a new colour range hits the fashion stores, it rapidly filters through to non-clothing items. However, it is a relatively small outlay to buy a T-shirt in this season's hottest shade, and it will not matter if you wear it for only three months. On the other hand, a big purchase, such as an armchair or sofa, is a different issue. You might also be tempted by this sort of item as a sale bargain, but it is not a good buy: it will look dated before the clocks change. This does not mean you have to choose something overly safe and classic. There are plenty of contemporary finishes around, but be aware that there is a world of difference between a modern look and a fashion fad. For the same reasons, avoid anything over-styled if you are spending a large sum. You might tire of it quickly, and it will not necessarily fit in if you move to another home.

STACKS AND SHELVES

Your home is your private domain and, as you probably spend a substantial length of time relaxing in your living room, it is appealing to personalize it with possessions and articles dotted around. Striking a balance between comfortable informality and clutter takes some thought. Books, for example, can look very attractive on shelves, and your choices can certainly reveal quite a bit about you, but those displayed should really be your most handsome hardbacks, rather than rows of untidy, tatty paperbacks. Store less-than-lovely titles on shelves with opaque glass doors, which will just give a hint of books behind them.

LOOK AND LISTEN

Videos, too, generally look ugly, and are best stored on shelves in a cupboard. These only need to be the width of a video-tape, and can have concertina-style doors, so the cupboard could slot in neatly behind a door, or even in an adjacent hallway or landing. There are plenty of storage choices in the shops for CDs, and many look quite smart and futuristic. A magazine rack is very useful for keeping papers under control, especially if your weekend ones tend to last seven days. Do be ruthless, though. After a week, tear out unread articles and recycle the rest. If you subscribe to and collect certain magazines, invest in good-quality magazine files, neatly labelled with the issue dates or volume numbers, and put them on show.

CHOSEN FEW

A mantelpiece can disappear beneath family photos, ornaments, postcards and invitations and the result is a total mishmash. Pare down to your real favourites, which you will then be able to appreciate properly, and don't hang on to out-of-date correspondence for the sake of it. Either file it or bin it, but clear it away. A few carefully chosen items look much stronger than hordes of bits. With decorative pieces, such as ceramics or candles, you can create a formal display by a symmetrical arrangement of pairs of items. If you want a looser, more natural feel, group together three comparable objects, perhaps balanced by a single one.

TAKE A REST

A living area is where you switch off after work and watch TV, where you throw a party for your friends, close your eyes to concentrate on music, wrestle with a cryptic crossword or spread Christmas presents, wrapping paper and string all over the floor. It is the backdrop to so much of your personal and social life. Make it the best venue you can.

modern lifestyle

FLEXIBLE LIVING

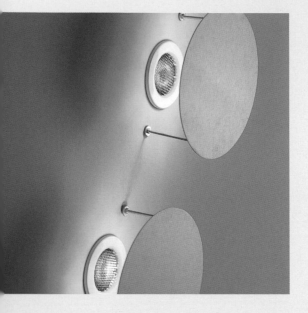

brave new world

Our world has altered more radically in the last ten years than in the preceding thirty, and we now enjoy a far less certain way of life than in the past. When you decide to make changes in your home, you might well be thinking only three or four years ahead, with a view to then revamping or moving house entirely.

People no longer automatically expect to stay in the same house from the day they marry until the day they die. The traditional 'job for life' is long gone and work opportunities often dictate relocation either here or abroad. We also upgrade or move more frequently as the investment value of property encourages us to regard a house as a financial asset.

As traditional patterns give way to new habits, the home evolves, too, meeting modern needs. A house designed a hundred years ago will naturally seem substantial compared to one built today. Families are now smaller, staff accommodation is virtually obsolete, and we no longer distinguish between rooms for every-day use and those saved exclusively for formal occasions. In addition, urban populations and increasing traffic continue to put pressure on living space.

Moving into the twenty-first century, we are often so busy and

DESIGN SOLUTIONS

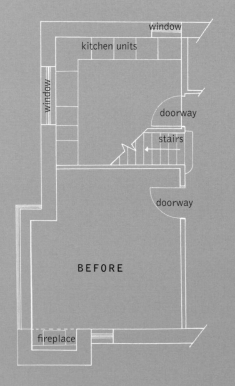

BEFORE

In the main living area of this modern house, a solid wall originally created two small, square spaces for the kitchen and living room. The stairs outside the kitchen door producing an enclosed feel and took up valuable floor space. The rooms seemed cramped, static and dull. The best feature, ripe for exploitation, was the height, almost double that normally expected.

Simply removing the central wall created a more open aspect. The kitchen was transferred to a mezzanine level and a dining area formed in its place, with a curved wall replacing the straight one. The central position of the spiral stairs leading to the mezzanine kitchen divided the seating and dining sectors without interrupting the view. The empty stairwell outside the room was converted into a small office (see page 36).

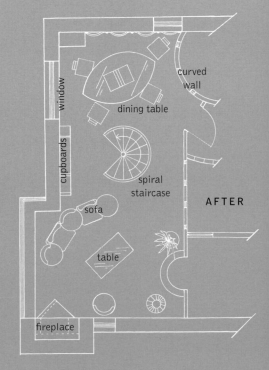

AFTER

fraught that home is a sanctuary where we yearn for a combination of simplicity, practicality and comfort. Streamlined design and handsome, low-maintenance materials have the right appeal for the future.

space it out

It has never been human nature to enjoy restricted space. We always prefer openness and at least an illusion of light and room to move, even if the reality is somewhat different. New homes often boast lots of 'extras' in the form of *en suite* showers or utility rooms, but these are generally quite tiny and can give the impression of a series of little boxes, particularly if ceilings are low, as is usually the case. A smaller home means multi-functional areas and demands being made on every inch, but there are ways to com-

bat a cramped and cluttered feeling.

Light is a key factor. If you block it out, you literally lose corners to darkness. Let it in and it illuminates the furthest extent of your area. Open-plan living emphasizes the sensation of light-filled space. Walls and partitions are obviously unavoidable at some points and desirable in others, but do seriously consider losing a wall that divides, for instance, a living room and a dining room. You will be able to see the total space unobstructed, which will help you to use it far more inventively. Don't ignore what's above your head or below you either. A mezzanine floor or central stairwell can provide a vista from the roof to the ground by letting light travel unimpeded the entire height of a building.

Where an internal partition is necessary, don't let it be just a boring barrier. Think laterally! It doesn't even have to be solid. You can install soft

lighting into a partition at a variety of levels, or create windows within it so that a glow from the next room shines through. Besides adding interest to a plain expanse, this also allows you to see from one space into another, indicating scope beyond the immediate boundaries. Take this concept a stage further, adding coloured glass illuminated by a fibre-optic in each narrow window. The effect is purely decorative, but gives a strong sense of another space nearby.

BOXED IN
Modern homes can be dispiriting, with their predictable, rectangular sections, featureless windows and lack of individuality. You need to add contrasting textures and shapes to bring the space alive. Curves, outlines inspired by nature and views from a variety of different levels bring a sense of freedom and motion, and again

Above left: Halogen spotlights can be used to bounce off a metal disc and give a subtle glow to a part of the room.

Right: A long, narrow slit cut into a wall allows a view into the next room, reinforcing a sense of further space. Purely decorative lighting on a wall can take the place of pictures or ornaments.

light can play a significant role in creating intriguing effects. Go for rounded silhouettes, especially for larger pieces of furniture against a straight wall, but punctuate the look with a couple of sharp angles or geometric forms. Each will enhance the impact of the other.

WONDER WALL

You might feel an empty wall increases the impression of space, but this does not always work. Making a feature, whether functional or simply for fun, gives meaning to that area, rather than leaving it to meld into blandness. There are plenty of alternatives to hanging pictures or photographs on the walls. Consider some of the fabulous light fittings now on the market, which are works of modern art in their own right. A woven wooden screen with a simple fluorescent tube behind it produces a sculptural, all-day com-

bination of texture, light and shadow play, as well as a backdrop for whatever activity takes place in that room.

CHIC SHELF

A shelf is an obvious item to hang on a wall, but it should not have to justify its prominent position by tidily storing lots of useful articles. You can locate your practical storage elsewhere and allow the shelf to be used indulgently – as a decorative showcase, perhaps.

If you plan to make something of a statement with a shelf, consider the item itself, as well as what what will be placed on it. In a light-coloured room, you can create an immediate harmonizing link between vertical and horizontal planes by using a contrasting darker stain for a wooden floor and wall unit. Make your shelf a substantial object in its own right, and let it span the full width or length of your area. If there is a window in the

middle, it can still run either side of it. Carefully pinpoint the right height on the wall. It should be at the average person's eye level so that the display can be appreciated without having to look up uncomfortably. At this position the whole structure will lead the eye across the room from one end to the other, drawing attention away from the typical less-than-lofty ceiling of a new house. The artefacts you pick for the shelf should have similarities in shape, colour or materials so that they form a homogeneous image. As a group, they form an intrinsic part of the finished scheme, so each one must be deliberately chosen.

WINDOW OF OPPORTUNITY

Far from being an attraction, the windows in some new homes can almost be an eyesore. They might be limited in size, badly positioned or, worst of all, just boring glass squares

Left: Interest is created on the wall through a variety of vertical and horizontal lines from the window frame and wall lights to free-standing items.

Right: Carefully chosen details can make or break a design. Style, depth and individuality are achieved through thoughtful touches, so spend some time finding exactly the right pieces and arrangements.

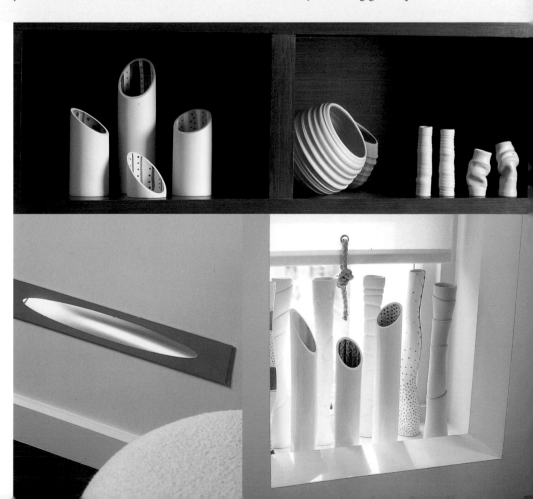

in the wall. If, no matter how much attention is lavished on them, they are never going to look good, you are better off disguising them, while still letting the daylight flood in. Neat blinds are a superb easy solution. Different glass finishes are an excellent alternative, too. For instance, you can cover a square window with two layers of Perspex, a coloured sheet, say, green, topped by an opaque one. The Perspex sheets can be cut into large circles and laid one on top of the other. These will overlap the window to lie against the wall. Daylight from behind will create an unexpected focal point, producing a panel of almost incandescent luminosity framed by a frosty sphere.

You can also think of a window as a blank picture, especially if the view from it is not too attractive. An empty canvas begs to be brought to life, framed and then admired for its own sake. Build a box-type surround for the window, painting it the same shade as the wall, so it appears almost part of the structure of the building. Add a toning blind if necessary, and then arrange a family of ceramic pieces on the window-sill to create a three-dimensional picture. Choose a variety of heights, shapes and textures, but a single colour or pattern.

MOVING PARTS

In a limited area you need few rather than lots of objects, leaving as much space around them as possible. You also want the greatest degree of flexibility so that the layout can be easily adapted to any situation. Above all, you need simple, comfortable pieces that function well and are visually in harmony with each other. Modular furniture is no longer the shiny vinyl horror of the 1970s, but part of the solution to making a twenty-first-century living room work for you. Soft, interlocking components that join seamlessly to make, for instance, an ample three-seater sofa, or break into a two-seater and separate chair, help you to rearrange the room and change the atmosphere to fit different occasions.

KEEP IT SIMPLE

Retain a streamlined look by not overloading furniture with piles of cushions. In the same way, choose fuss-free blinds that blend with the rest of the room rather than attract attention, not to mention dust. Don't be afraid of creating a clinical environment: it can be made welcoming. A fireplace, for instance, can fit in easily if you devote a little thought to the look. Opt for a

Left: Although the fire is not the focal point, a circular seating arrangement around it still creates a cosy atmosphere in this part of the room.

contemporary style in a natural material such as slate or flagstone.

Stick to smooth flooring for the entire area; a rug will destroy that precious sense of spaciousness. Bamboo is an option that will become increasingly familiar in the home of the future. It is comfortable, tough, sustainable and easily wipes clean. A deep, high-shine woodstain is an effective foil for light-coloured walls, introducing warmth without loss of definition. A dark carpet would, like a rug, absorb light and shrink the room. A glossy floor will always reflect light, no matter how dark the shade.

modern manners

Letting one room double for two or even three purposes is an everyday occurrence as a consequence of smaller homes and a more compact lifestyle. The numbers of people working from home for at least part of the week mean that many of us have to squeeze an office into our living space.

The separate dining room is the most obvious casualty of this downsizing. Eating now generally takes place either in the kitchen or sitting room, and is often a solitary activity, as mealtimes are no longer automatically the family gatherings they once were.

Fortunately, furniture manufacturers are producing a greater choice of pieces scaled to meet current needs. The banqueting board has been superseded by a neat dining table, round or oval, and probably adjustable for either a couple or a party. A single diner could eat conveniently while chatting with a partner relaxing on the sofa. Today's materials are glass, aluminium and wood. Surfaces are sleek and shapes are fluid, in keeping with the drive for crispness and simplicity.

Right and below: Even the smallest fireplace can have character. Tucked into a corner, flagstones create a surround that is both functional and dynamic. In this instance, the chimney breast is on the outside of the house, which leaves a flush inside wall.

home office

MAKE SPACE WORK FOR YOU

Above: A screen of rippling, jigsawed plywood gives a softness to a blank corner.

every home should have one

Even if you don't do it yourself, you are almost certain to know someone who does – work from home that is. The ranks of the self-employed continue to grow, and it is now common practice for staff to operate from a dedicated phone and computer within their own four walls for at least part of the week. Pressures of work are such that many jobs make demands beyond the hours of nine to five, or Monday to Friday, so people put in extra time during the evenings or at weekends. You might not be in this situation, but perhaps you would like an area for a home computer. More and more people are gaining access to the Internet and looking to the future when banking, shopping and paying bills will all be done in this way. You need a place for this facility.

If you fall into any of these categories, it is essential to take the concept of a home office seriously and create an area that is tailored to those specific needs. It is not just about having somewhere to sit with a keyboard and phone. If you are dealing with your livelihood, you must adopt the right frame of mind. It is both unhealthy and unproductive to

DESIGN SOLUTIONS

There was a cavernous stairwell outside the living room (of the house referred to on page 30), a huge void begging to be utilized. This task was accomplished more easily than might be expected. Flooring and a partition wall were constructed on supporting wooden beams fixed across the space. Then the main living room wall was knocked through and replaced by an additional partition wall. The result was a small office, reached via two steps up from the living area. The change in level was not essential, but created a sense of a separate zone. A doorway without a door also divided home from work whilst maintaining an open aspect. Sunshine flooded in from a skylight, supplemented by light from semi-circular glass inserts in the wall, which also allowed a view out to the landing, giving the impression of a larger space.

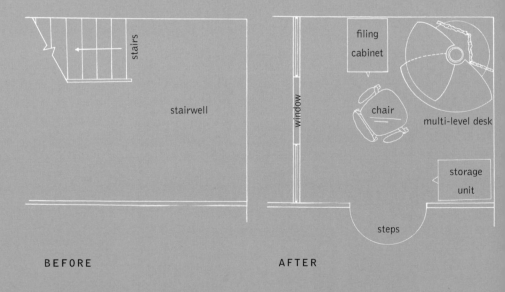

BEFORE

AFTER

try to work in a badly arranged space. You are not likely to achieve much perched on the bed with a folder on your knee.

FILES OR FRIENDS?

Deciding where to locate your office can be problematic. If you have a spare bedroom, this might appear to be the ideal spot. You could put a desk in the corner, store stationery on the window-sill, and even use the bed for spreading out your files. When your aunt comes for her annual weekend visit, you could easily shove it all into the wardrobe…really?

Make your home work for you and your needs. The hours you spend at work will massively outweigh the amount of time guests stay, even if you entertain every weekend of the year. If you have the luxury of a spare room, devote it to your work. For true peace of mind, your everyday job must

take precedence over occasional entertaining. Make your office a place where guests can be put up from time to time, rather than struggle to forge your career surrounded by duvets and dressing tables.

PRIME SITES

It is probable that you have no spare bedrooms, and will need, therefore, to adapt part of your home. When you are considering the siting of an office, look at every possibility. Is there a wasted corner under the stairs, or in an attic conversion? What about putting a bed up on supports, creating scope for a desk below? If you normally sit down to work, you will not need a lot of headroom, so these kinds of spots could be perfect. Alternatively, you might be able to section off part of a living room or kitchen.

Below: Wherever you can see from one room into another, it is vital to ensure that the two designs are complementary in colour and look.

Right and below: This tiny office has a skylight but no windows to provide any sense of space beyond, so semi-circular glass panes in the wall break up the solid barrier. Without these, the office would seem claustrophobic and box-like.

WORKER'S RIGHTS

Wherever you decide to put the office, you cannot do without the following elements.

- You must have good light for all tasks. If you are peering at a screen for any length of time, you will end up with eye strain and headaches, not to mention neck and back problems. Natural light from behind a computer screen is the best, and a directional desk lamp is essential if you are burning the midnight oil.
- You might need a fax machine, computer, printer, desk lamp, radio, CD player and other electrical items, so give yourself plenty of power points. If necessary, have a few extra put in, rather than muddle through with adaptors. Remember, you might want to add new pieces of equipment in the future, so a spare socket is unlikely to go to waste. If you are running a business from home, at least one spare phone line is also a good idea.
- Get yourself a proper desk, with room for a computer, drawers for stationery and whatever else you need to do your work comfortably and efficiently. The latest 'work-stations' consist of a pole with modular shelving branching off, which gives surface room at a range of levels convenient for a keyboard, phone or lamp.
- Buy the very best chair you can afford. You will probably be sitting on it for far longer each day than on your sofa, so you should be looking to spend a similar amount on each. It sounds extravagant, but it is an investment you will be glad you made.

SECTION LEADER

Motivation can be a real problem for the home-based worker. It is all too easy to be distracted by your 'other' life when you do not have the discipline of the office, and colleagues to focus you. The surroundings you work in should encourage concentration and put you into a 'professional' frame of mind. If you operate from a corner of the living room or kitchen, it is really helpful to give the work-place some sense of being separate from the rest of the home. You could put up a partition, with a doorway cut into it, but no actual door. This saves space and allows you to see from one part of the area into the other, so you do not feel penned in. An even simpler solution is to use a screen to section off the office area. A change of level can be all that is needed, so a situation where you step up or down within the room to reach your desk can also be successful.

Right: This layered desk maximizes space and looks forward to the paper-free office of the future.

Below: Opt for extra electrical sockets. Stylish materials rather than utilitarian plastic will make the office seem more home-like.

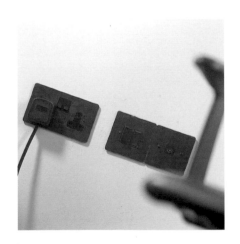

TOP MANAGEMENT

Aside from missing all the stress of commuting, or dealing with an impossible boss, one of the many advantages of working at home is that you can make your office as pleasant and home-like as you wish. In fact, the more you like it, the longer you will want to spend there.

Part of its appeal will stem from how conveniently you can work in it. As with any other part of your home, you should plan by asking yourself what is required from the space. Visualize a typical day at work, and think through how you use all your equipment and what needs to be to hand for each task. Work out how much storage you need for papers, books, samples or other articles, and do not forget to check the heights of files so that you allow enough room on shelves for them to stand upright.

If you can see into your office from another part of your home, look into fitting doors on to shelves to conceal files and work-related items. Apart from the privacy angle, it is really important that you relax after hours. If you catch sight of a mountain of paperwork from your sofa, or when you are eating, it is going to spoil any attempt to switch off from your job. For the same reason, separate phone numbers for work contacts and friends can be a godsend. Depending on the nature of your business, you might not want to receive professional calls in the evenings or at weekends. An answering machine on your work number will take care of these calls, leaving you informed but undisturbed.

DOMESTIC DETAILS

Small touches can make a huge difference to how you feel when working at home. Treat yourself to colourful, interesting stationery and equipment you just wouldn't see in the average impersonal office. Choose a calculator, stapler and pens that you like, rather than typical company-issue types. Good-looking storage baskets will perform as well as ugly, functional plastic crates, and will bring a more relaxing, softer edge to your environment. Install some smart slate or chrome electrical sockets instead of utilitarian plastic squares, and banish harsh fluorescent strip-lighting in favour of clear halogens and a good desk-lamp. Share the office with fresh flowers or a healthy, dust-free houseplant. The beauty of the home office is that it can combine order and efficiency with comfort and pleasure. It should give you the best of both worlds.

Right: A sense of wholeness comes from the continuation of the bamboo flooring from the living room into the office.

Below: The home office gives you an opportunity to personalize your work area with good-looking and out-of-the-ordinary details and fittings.

the feel-good factor

flat earth

The richness of our world is revealed to us through our five senses, of which the dominant one is sight. When you are planning a living room, your first question will most likely be, 'What colours do I want?' Colour has instant visual impact, provoking immediate reactions, so once you have picked your shades, you might feel the job is all but completed. However, if you explore no further, the result will be dull and insubstantial, lacking character and depth. Something is missing.

Imagine creating a room in which you can have absolutely any furniture, fabrics, lighting and accessories you wish. The one thing you are forbidden is colour. Without this aspect, how do you begin to introduce drama, style and atmosphere?

There is a single element that will breathe life into any space, colourful or neutral, large or small, functional or decorative. Texture is one of the most powerful, evocative and versatile tools at a designer's disposal, but it is a factor that is often forgotten, or skimmed over unthinkingly. Harness it and you have the key to stimulating and ultimately more satisfying surroundings.

REACH OUT AND TOUCH

It is human nature to want to touch things. Think of a young baby

DESIGN SOLUTIONS

This conversion flat in a Victorian house had a typically prominent bay window and central fireplace flanked by shelves. Brimming with messy books right up to the ceiling, the shelves gave the room a cluttered feel, emphasized by the gloomy walls and flooring. The object of this exercise was to achieve a cosmetic transformation, so major structural changes were not considered.

The room was completely emptied and the shelves removed, so that the fixed space could be assessed. Cupboards, built at knee-height along the wall in front and to the side of the fire, provided more storage space than the shelves had done. The top of the cupboards, covered in white cobbles, acted as a hearth for the fireplace. In keeping with the design, a sleek, sliding glass door replaced the conventional one. The whole room was decorated and furnished in shades of white, but using a range of textures.

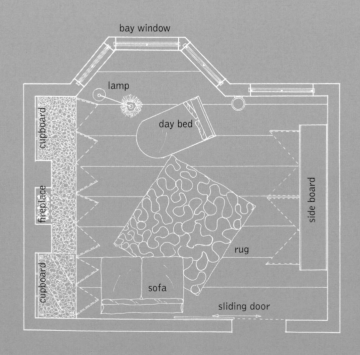

absorbed in an everyday object, such as a wooden spoon. She will constantly turn and finger it and even use her mouth to learn all she can about its surface. This desire to investigate through the sense of touch never leaves us. We always want go further than simply looking. We try to involve ourselves, to experience everything our environment has to offer. Our skin alerts us to innumerable sensations as we continually brush against and handle metals, powders, fabrics, liquids and even animals and plants in the course of a single day.

Yet, extraordinarily, this facet of design is often virtually ignored when we are planning our homes, usually with less than inspiring results. So, go against the flow, put colour to one side for a moment and reawaken your sense of touch. Texture is doubly satisfying because it feeds two senses – sight and touch – simultaneously.

Above left: Textured rugs, such as this one, will give a floor an added dimension.

Above right: A hearth need not be a flat stone slab. A spread of cobbles is equally fireproof, but far more interesting.

Right: Fabric-covered hardboard squares both look and feel luxurious and can be effective in disguising less-than-perfect plaster.

Just looking at an adorable fluffy kitten makes you want to bury your face in its fur. You do not need to run your hand over a concrete wall to know that it is abrasive and unyielding. You can appreciate surface detail as easily as colour, and it tells you what to expect when you put out your hand. The visual quality of texture is really a taster before the best part, when you actually make contact.

One hand on that concrete wall tells you all you need to know about harsh functionality. The kitten, on the other hand, with its warm silkiness, evokes feelings of comfort and contentment. The sense of touch reaches our emotions and is a powerful means of creating mood. At the end of a stressful day nestle into plump, squashy cushions on a velvety sofa and feel your tension float away. Stride into a fuss-free kitchen of cold, shiny steel

and smooth, unyielding tiles and you are immediately fired with single-minded efficiency.

surface success

The most exciting textural effects are achieved by contrast. Think of a flat painted floor, firm and cool under foot. Throw down a plain-coloured rug with a luxurious, embossed pattern and you immediately create sensuality and interest. Lay the dense matt finish of fake suede fabric next to pearly satin and enjoy the interplay of sheen and weave. Watch how natural light on a floor or wall picks out a subdued pattern of matt and gloss finishes. Simple tricks like these can go a long way to pepping up a dull interior, and accessorizing with a few well-considered items will make a difference.

You can take this concept a stage further, juxtaposing objects of contrasting nature as well as texture – a rough vase of ancient lava brimming with delicate lilies which will fade in a matter of days, or inanimate pebbles heaped around a flickering fire. Thoughtful touches such as these bring definition and character into your home.

SOFTLY, SOFTLY

By prioritizing tactile rather than visual elements you will throw up possibilities far beyond the introduction of a few interesting fabrics and rugs. You can transform key areas, such as walls, doors and floors, in ways that make you itch to touch them. Take texture this far and you will probably notice some more subtle effects you might not have considered. Imagine yourself in an Alpine valley after a very heavy snowfall. Apart from not being able to

Left: The similarity in material of these vases creates a homogenous group.

Above: This frivolously fluffy light is there to be touched and admired as well as for its function.

Right: The unexpected swooping shape of the fireplace is a foil for the square forms of the tiles and wall panels.

see a great deal, you might well be struck by the utter silence around you. Deep snow muffles sound and you can capture something of its calming and insulating qualities. Tiles with a matt finish will bring a chalky, almost absorbent quality to walls, as will velvets and fake suedes. Grainy, semi-opaque glass can add to a cocoon-like feel, while deep-pile rugs, fun fur and knobbly knits will take the sharp edges off furniture and flooring. Compare this atmosphere of comfort and safety to the harsh, unwelcoming experience of entering a room where sounds echo and vibrate discordantly off hard surfaces.

COLOUR CHANGE

Although the colour of a fabric, tile or paint finish is what first grabs your attention, it is the detail on its surface that gives individuality and life. Imagine three cushions all dyed exactly the same shade of rich chocolate brown. One is made of plain, regularly woven cotton, one is a slubby raw silk with a subtle shine and the third is a plush corduroy. The cotton one would seem drab, utilitarian and completely unappealing, while the other two would have the nearest thing that exists to cushion charisma. You would long to pick them up and stroke them rather than sit on them. This is one of the games texture can play with you, totally changing the appearance of an item, regardless of colour, lending subtlety to the most garish tones and glamour to the dullest.

Paler colours often work more successfully as backdrops because they reflect more light and therefore show up contours more strongly. Textures can also evoke associations and

rekindle memories. Plastics in fuchsia pink, acid yellow and deep purple belong firmly in the Western world of the 1960s. Transpose those exact shades on to hand-woven silk saris and they have graced the women of India for generations. Bring a sparkling, metallic finish to scarlet and forest green and you'll think of Christmas. Change the surface to a soft, fleecy fabric and the outdoor world of mountaineering and hill-walking come to mind.

THE LIGHTEST TOUCH

The textural effects you can create are almost unlimited, but to enjoy them fully you will need to maximize that initial visual impact so that the desire to touch becomes irresistible. To appreciate detail properly you need to use lighting in a way that brings out its beauty and complexity. This will by no means involve the brightest, clearest possible lighting.

Three-dimensional planes demand subtle light and shadow, which emphasize contours, rather than bold illumination, which would only flatten and dilute interest. Light can be directed to rebound off so many different surfaces and is a vital means of showing off the visual aspects of a multitude of textures.

final touch

The potential for variety and interest, which our sense of touch represents, is almost infinite. Consider it seriously as a means of producing a truly comfortable, relaxing and inspiring environment and you might start wondering why textures have been out of the spotlight for so long. Now is your chance to reach out and make up for lost time.

Above: A circular hole at the centre of the design acts as an uncomplicated handle, which does not interfere with the look of the glass door.

Left: A ribbed spiral radiator complements the ribbed fabric at the window. Plenty of imaginatively styled heating appliances are now available if you make time to search out the sources.

Right: Side boards are back in fashion! The newest pieces are utterly simple in style and finish. Details such as white covers on the books are essential to the overall scheme.

the light stuff

LIGHT FOR LIVING

lights up!

Light dictates quite literally how you see a room. It influences how you use it and even how it makes you feel. You are obliged to allow for its changing moods during a single day and throughout the year. Such a powerful medium needs to be considered alongside colour, upholstery, furniture and flooring, yet more often than not when we decorate, it is way down our list of priorities. Turn the spotlight on to this aspect, and you will reveal a cache of brilliant effects, both highly practical and indulgently decorative.

IN THE DARK

Working out lighting is not easy. It does not seem to come naturally to most of us, mainly because we have very little experience of well-lit areas. Sadly, most homes in the UK are lighting catastrophes, where supposedly relaxing spaces, such as the living room, shake you alert with their startling brightness, and kitchens are filled with harsh shadow from gloomy and buzzing fluorescent strips. Offices, shops and public buildings are generally illuminated for function rather than atmosphere, and it can be hard to put your finger on just what is creating the ideal ambience in a thoughtfully lit restaurant.

Above: The centre is by no means the only position for ceiling lighting. Coloured bulbs add a further dimension to the effects you can create.

Buying lighting can be a minefield. Shops often have scant information on all the various types; you might not have the opportunity to switch lamps on and off; and the shops themselves can be so dazzling that it is impossible to see the effect of a single item.

Bearing all this in mind, the route to success is careful research and planning. Don't let lighting become an afterthought purchased in a rush when everything else is in place. It is a vital component of your design, so treat it this way and you will get the best from the room. Neglect it and much of your effort will go unnoticed.

BROAD SPECTRUM

It pays to think initially about what you want to be able to do in your room. Flexibility is the key, as most areas have more than one function. Clear, even lighting in a kitchen is essential for performing tasks without casting your own shadow over the work area. You will also want the option of a softer, more relaxing effect if you are eating in the kitchen as well.

The living room is where lighting has to be the most flexible, accommodating the variety of activities you perform here. You'll need a directional, possibly mobile light source for reading, a medium-level glow for watching television or chatting with friends, and something stronger for, say, finding that lost contact lens.

COUNT THE COST

As you think through your lighting plan, it is essential to cost out what you need to buy. Lamps and fittings can be surprisingly expensive, so don't underestimate. There are some incredibly stylish pieces available and a light source can become the focal point of a living room, with the rest of the scheme built around it, so it's worth saving up to get exactly the right item. Transforming run-of-the-mill lighting into a real display need not mean rewiring your entire room. You can make a tremendous difference by just reconsidering how existing power points could be used.

SOURCES MADE SIMPLE

Listed below are the main kinds of lighting available for domestic use.
FLUORESCENT LIGHTING This is available in tubes, rings and other compact shapes. It gives a bright, even light and does not get hot, so it can be boxed, and is the best choice for kitchen worktops. It is unflattering as a main light because it drains definition and creates greyness. However, it is economical and long-lasting.
TUNGSTEN LIGHTING Standard light-bulbs, which give out a yellow-toned light; can be combined with a dimmer switch. The bulbs are available

Far left: Ceiling lights are often too meagre in scale, but a simple, perforated wooden casing makes a spectacular and inexpensive fitting.

Left: Day or night, this clock-face projection adds drama to the dining area.

LEVEL LIGHTING

The easiest way to think about where to install lighting is to visualize five distinct levels that require a light source. They are the floor (Level 1), somewhere around your waist height (Level 2), chest height (Level 3), head height (Level 4) and ceiling (Level 5). Each level requires a specific type of illumination.

- LEVEL 1 A glow coming up from the floor will produce atmosphere for entertaining or just relaxing, and can also be positioned to highlight a particular object or feature.
- LEVEL 2 At waist height you will probably need a table-lamp, perhaps near hi-fi equipment, or by a phone where you might need to make notes.
- LEVEL 3 At chest level you will want an adjustable, directional light for reading. It could be floor-standing, or an Anglepoise type of lamp on a table.
- LEVEL 4 The main ambient light in your room will originate at head height, possibly from a wall-mounted or free-standing uplighter fitted with a dimmer switch.
- LEVEL 5 From the ceiling you can, if necessary, fill the room with light for a task, but add a dimmer switch to minimize any harsh effects.

Above: The floor is not an obvious place to introduce lighting, but with the guidance of an experienced electrician it is entirely possible and practical. The results can be stunning.

in different colours, with or without pearlized finishes, or partially silvered to create a diffused glow or directional beam for reading.

HALOGEN LIGHTING Small natural or coloured bulbs that can be fitted flush to ceilings, under shelves or inside cabinets. They give a crisp light, similar to daylight, so are useful in a kitchen for tasks such as chopping and preparing food. Choose sealed units for safety in any damp atmosphere. A transformer must usually be fitted with halogen bulbs, although integral transformers are now available. Halogen lighting is more expensive than tungsten, and not always compatible with a dimmer switch.

FANTASTIC FIBRES

Although they are not suitable as a main light source, fibre-optics are becoming increasingly popular for purely decorative lighting. Apart from their mesmerizingly magical effect, the beauty of them is that there are no bulbs to blow, so they can continue to produce the most spectacular show, day or night, from quite inaccessible places, never needing to be disturbed. An uninteresting living room can be transformed by a below-the-floor installation of fibre-optics, producing a sparkling new take on rugs or painted floorboards. They are a safe and brilliant way to create a light-show in a child's room, as they also remain completely cool. There is no electricity in the fibres themselves, so they can combine safely with water, and are ideal for outside use. Imagine a water feature glittering in a night-time garden, or tiny points of light marking out a path. Fit fibre-optics around the edge of a bath or Jacuzzi, or even into a shower-head and you will be truly bathed in light. Always use a qualified electrician to install fibre-optics.

PLAY IT SAFE

We all know that electricity is dangerous stuff, but in amateur hands it can be lethal. A qualified electrician must be an indispensable part of your budget. Spend less on lamps if you have to, but never compromise on safety.

- Areas of high humidity, such as kitchens and bathrooms, hold particular risks as water and electricity can be a fatal combination. Your electrician will know how to cross-bond the pipework to ensure that all exposed metal, such as the cooker or bath, is earthed. This ensures that if any wiring becomes damaged, it cannot cause appliances to become live and therefore deadly.
- Choose sealed lighting units, where no metal parts are exposed, or fittings that completely enclose a bulb. A splash of water can cause a hot light-bulb to shatter.
- Bathroom lights should be controlled by a pull-cord inside the room, or by a switch outside.
- In the kitchen, where the dangers of sharp objects and hot surfaces are obvious, good lighting will help to prevent accidents.

Bear in mind the following rules for personal safety.

- Never touch any electrical equipment with wet hands.
- Avoid trailing flexes. Young children could pull a lamp or appliance down on to themselves, or you could trip up.
- Replace frayed flexes or broken plugs as soon as you notice them.
- Switch the power off at the mains before starting any electrical tasks.
- Don't overload sockets.
- Whenever you move house, no matter what age your new home is, have the wiring thoroughly checked by a qualified electrician. Don't just take the word of the builder or previous owner. This goes for newly built properties as well as older ones.
- If in any doubt whatsoever, call expert help.

GLITTERING PRIZES

Obviously, good lighting is essential if a room is to function efficiently but, if you are looking for originality, real style and an element of surprise, you must exploit its decorative potential. As a designer's tool, light has an advantage over paint, wallpaper and fabric in that it does not need to be permanent. You can switch it on or off, alter surrounding colours by using different coloured bulbs, and move the light sources around to create ever-changing effects on floors, ceilings or walls. A plain, cream-painted sitting room that looks fresh and simple by day but lifeless in the evening can be transformed by clever lighting.

Innovative lighting can produce a temporary work of art at the flick of a switch. You can wake up a blank wall with beams from blue-toned halogen lights fringing the ceiling above and tilted to shine just above picture-rail height. A snow-white cornice can be transformed into a golden glow by using a length of rope lighting to pick out its complexity. You can cast a spell over a bedroom, bathroom or living area with flickering firelight and simple candles, or experiment with projections on to plain walls by day as well as by night.

Remember, the light itself is only half the story. Contrast is at the heart of ingenious lighting, and patches of shadow or darkness will serve to enhance the picture.

EARTHLY POWERS

Alongside artificial light in all its forms, don't overlook the potential of natural light. True, you can't control or shape it in quite the same way, but as it will come streaming into your home whether you wish it to or not, it's worth thinking about ways of harnessing it. On a sunny day you can create wonderful shadow-play with a venetian blind, or atmospheric dappled light through a roller-blind perforated in the right places. Voile curtains produce a restful, filmy haze, while daylight passing through cut or coloured glass will scatter rainbow fragments wherever it strikes.

BRIGHT FUTURE

Perfecting lighting is tricky. It takes effort, planning and some trial and error, not to mention your hard-earned money. But why spend time and resources decorating and furnishing a room if it cannot be properly appreciated, and fulfil all your needs? Only with the most thoughtful lighting will a room look, feel and function as you intended. Only when you are content with the character at any time of day or night can you be sure that the light is right.

Right: These illuminated picture frames illustrate how light can be harnessed to create interest at any time of day.

Below: Flexible rope lighting, inserted above a picture rail all round the perimeter of a room, highlights ceiling details simply and effectively and creates a soft glow.

kitchen and
dining spaces

The kitchen is probably the room about which you have the most fixed ideas. When you start to plan alterations in here, you will most likely have a style in mind – maybe a country kitchen, with bunches of dried herbs hanging from beams, or a shiny, steel set-up brimming with efficiency. Stop right there…

Kitchens are working rooms. Nowhere else in your home do you carry out as many practical tasks. Aside from preparing food, you will wash up, maybe iron clothes, make small repairs, write lists and perform a host of other chores. An inconvenient layout, poor lighting (see In the Dark, page 46) and shortage of power points or storage areas will drive you to distraction. To make a success of redesigning a kitchen, you must erase all thoughts of style and look from your mind, and concentrate first and fully on function.

FREQUENTLY FORGOTTEN

- Plan for that microwave! Incorporate it into your design or it will end up filling valuable space on your worktop.
- A rubbish bin is part of a working kitchen and does not need concealing, but it needs to be out of the way, yet still handy for your cooking areas.
- Corner cupboards with conventional shelving inside are really not much use. Insist on efficient carousel shelves.
- You own all the space between the floor and the ceiling, so use every bit. Wall units and shelves can go right up to the ceiling. But make sure you can still reach regularly used items without having to climb a ladder every time you need them.
- Keep order, particularly under the sink, with pull-out baskets instead of shelves. You will make the best use of this space if you can easily see and reach what is there.
- Don't make lighting your last thought. You will need flexible sources for tasks, socializing and eating, so investigate worktop lights, overhead spots and wall-lights on a dimmer-switch.

Planning is the key to success in most projects, and redesigning your kitchen is no exception. It might sound boring, but it is essential to be disciplined. You are making important and costly decisions, so base them on sound research. Set aside sufficient time, maybe a month or longer, to look into all the options available (see Heaps and Hoards, page 12). Rushed choices could irritate you for years to come, so don't be tempted to part with a penny until you have chosen every last piece of the jigsaw from flooring to light fittings. Each component will have a knock-on effect to something else, so make sure they all sit together comfortably before you commit yourself.

MONEY MATTERS

Be absolutely realistic about the financial implications of your plans (see Mind Your Money, page 14). Changing a kitchen is a daunting undertaking because this is the most expensive room in your home to fit out. Whatever your limit, you will thank yourself later on if you spend only about three-quarters of it. There will always be unforeseen problems and the rest of your money is virtually guaranteed to disappear on sorting these out. If you don't allow a reasonable safety-net, you might end up with a glorious kitchen where you serve nothing but cheese sandwiches for months.

It is vital at this stage to be completely honest with yourself about what you really want to achieve. Try not to get caught up in the look of your room, but concentrate first on its purposes. Cosmetic details of colour and style can, and should, come later. Work out what your priorities truly are. Why invest money and space in an industrial-sized steel cooker with no room for a microwave if you eat prepared meals six nights out of seven? Changing your room will not alter your personality or daily habits, so grasp the opportunity to fulfil your real needs. You will feel properly relaxed only if your home reflects you, not someone you would like to be.

EASY PIECES

Kitchen planning is a complex business. If you feel overwhelmed and don't know where to begin, the simplest way to demystify the task is to take it step by step. Break it down into manageable chunks. For instance, you might want to start by thinking about the essentials, such as gas, electricity and water supplies. Where should these be located? How many power points or water inlets will you need? Can existing ones be used? At this stage you will need to call in your experts, such as a plumber and electrician, so have these contacts thought out, too. (See page 20 for tips on forming a team.)

SKETCHY IDEAS

Follow the same steps that you would for planning any other space. Focus on what you have to work with by drawing a scale diagram, complete with any fixtures such as windows, doors or a fireplace (see Picture This, page 9). Then start planning your layout. You might need to make as many as a dozen rough sketches of your design, which can then be honed down to about six choices. Spend some time fleshing out each of these, until you eliminate all but the best solution. Work out the essentials, such as places for your cooker, washing-machine and dishwasher, and also how many units or shelves you will need. Assuming that you are redesigning an existing kitchen, be guided by what you had to start with. Was it enough or too little? What would you like more of?

TAPE AND SHAPES

Paper shapes, cut to scale to represent your furniture, can be moved around on your flat plan to find the best layout. Another effective way is to

These are some of the questions you should answer before confirming your design.

- Should cupboards open from the left or right, and the oven door be hinged at the bottom or the side? If on the side, which side?
- Can you move comfortably around the furniture to reach all areas?
- Are your fridge, hob, bin and sink positioned conveniently to minimize the distance you have to walk between them?
- Have you allowed enough work surfaces and power points for essentials, such as the kettle and toaster?
- Do you need somewhere for a notice-board, telephone and writing surface?

create a life-sized plan by marking out the positions of furniture and appliances on the floor with masking tape so you can clearly see whether they are practical. Obviously, the fewer items there are in the room the easier this is, so it might not be appropriate unless you are working in an empty area. Keep the purpose of each item at the forefront of your mind, and try not to become sidetracked by the cosmetic details early on. Remember, a kitchen has to fulfil several vital functions every day, and you will achieve a far more satisfying result if you invest at least as much time in the practicalities of layout as you do in its appearance.

When you are happy with the plan, ask yourself, 'What am I gaining from my design and will the space now fulfil my needs?' If you don't like the answers, think again.

SALES TALK

When given your room's dimensions, any of the large kitchen manufacturers will be able to computerize a rough sketch, produce a scale diagram and

Above: Fruit can be as decorative in the kitchen as plants or cut flowers, and of course it's edible too. Pay attention to details such as the choice of bowl.

finishing touches

Once you are totally satisfied with the practicalities and functioning of the kitchen, you can allow yourself to consider decoration. Colour is an obvious aspect to look at. Typical 'kitchen' colours tend to be the fresh blues and greens with their associations of water and vegetation. There are no rules, however, so don't ignore more subtle palettes such as taupes, or heathers and mauves. Less commonly seen shades, such as pink, can also work surprisingly well in the right surroundings, so keep an open mind. If you choose white for the walls, units in any other colour might appear to dominate, yet too much white will create a rather clinical feel, so use it with caution. A slight shift to cream will result in a softer, more homely effect.

It is rare today for a room to have a single function. With our ongoing need to use our homes efficiently, the days of the separate dining room are really over. Preparing and enjoying meals all in one place makes far more sense. Decoration plays a big part in designating areas for, say, cooking and entertaining, without 'sectioning off' bits too rigidly. A change of colour or style of décor can indicate a different zone, without the need for a physical boundary.

suggest layouts and types of units. This can be very helpful as long as you take the sketch home and consider it in your own time, away from the pressure of the sales floor. You can pick up valuable tips in this way, but do bear in mind that the staff are there to sell you as much kitchen paraphernalia as possible.

PACE THE FLOOR

As you formulate your design, you need to be confident that it will work in practice. This is particularly important in a kitchen where you will be carrying out many daily tasks, probably with very little space to spare. You will be very frustrated in the future if a drawer will open fully only if you move a chair first, or if you have to keep trekking from the hob to the sink via the washing-machine and wine-rack. The only way to test your plan is to pretend to perform your regular tasks. You might feel completely ridiculous pacing from the imaginary oven to the invisible sink, or opening the door of the non-existent fridge, but swallow your embarrassment and do it. It will highlight vital questions that are easily overlooked.

FAB FLOORS FOR KITCHENS

The flooring material is a vital component of any room. In the kitchen it has to be non-slip, easily cleaned and hard-wearing. Wood, tiles or a vinyl-type flooring are automatic suggestions, but look beyond these for alternatives, which will set your floor apart. In each instance there are pros and cons, so research well and weigh up how far you want to compromise practicalities for style. Consider:
SEALED CONCRETE A budget option if you feel comfortable with a fiercely industrial look. Totally unforgiving, of course, if you drop glass or china on to it. It can also easily be painted and there are great factory-type floor colours available, from functional

to fashionable. The concrete needs to be extremely smooth in order to look good. Any roughness will be uncomfortable to walk on, and could trip you up.

BAMBOO Environmentally friendly as it regrows in three to five years, compared to a tree, which can take thirty to forty years. Bamboo is extremely tough and will not warp, so it is practical for every room. Available in lots of different stains, it is comparable to a wood laminate floor in terms of price.

RUBBER AND SPORTS FLOORINGS An uncommon choice, but worth investigating. Sports flooring has plenty of bounce and a good grip, so it is safe and very comfy under foot. It is available in some stunning bright colours, but would be an expensive choice for a large area. Rubber flooring has similar properties and can be fitted to overlap the plinth of a unit, acting as a seal. Scuff marks can be noticeable, and strong sunlight might cause the rubber to perish over time.

INDUSTRIAL METAL Hard, cool and a bit noisy under foot. Treadplate sheets can be cut into manageable tiles and screwed down. For the seriously style-conscious only.

LIQUID TERRAZZO Widely used in commercial buildings, this flooring is formed from wet cement, pigmented to any shade. Before the cement sets, marble and/or granite chips are laid in, either at random to produce a speckled effect or in a pattern. When hardened, the surface is highly polished. You can pick your own colour combination and, unlike tiling, there are no joins. Check that a non-slip process can be applied.

HEAVILY SANDBLASTED GLASS Can be installed as a raised, semi-opaque floor, or laid as tiles on to an utterly flat sub-surface. Variations in sandblasting can produce pattern and also increase non-slip quality. Call in an expert.

DOWN TO BASICS

Furniture can quickly fill up a small kitchen, leaving no space to move around. Whichever items you are considering, ask yourself honestly whether they are the most practical and useful choices. You might crave a country-style dresser decked out with pretty plates, but does your china really merit such attention? Is your kitchen the right spot for decorative displays? More often than not, dressers just accumulate all sorts of bits and pieces, such as postcards, buttons and souvenirs. Any plates on show need washing regularly as they pick up all the dust and grease in the air. Unless your kitchen is very large and spacious, a dresser will prevent you having enough good cupboard space, which means you will end up with a frustrating and impractical kitchen.

The key to accentuating spaciousness is to let in as much light as possible, so choose furniture and fittings carefully, avoiding anything chunky or solid-looking. Go for clean lines and smooth, semi-translucent surfaces. Pick pieces with slim legs which allow light on to walls and the floorspace beneath them and which do not take up unnecessary room. Think practicality: can your chairs be easily stacked and stored? Can your table expand to accommodate extra guests? Do handles protrude, interfering with the line of your cupboards?

SHOP AROUND

The choice of appliances available is amazing, as are the price differentials that you'll no doubt come across. If you are looking for a basic piece of equipment, such as a fridge-freezer, you will probably want a certain capacity and maybe a few specific features, such as a drinks dispenser. Beyond that, there is little to choose between the many brands on the market, yet you can, if you wish, pay double or even more for a supposedly 'upmarket' name than for a less well-renowned one. Unbiased consumer literature can be a helpful guide to reliability, but the most sensible course is to ignore the brand labels and choose the best-priced model that fulfils your needs. Don't forget to fill in and return guarantees straight away, otherwise they will disappear. Extended warranties are generally too expensive to be worthwhile. Remember that today's kitchen appliances usually have built-in obsolescence and will need to be replaced after a certain number of years.

EVERYTHING BUT...

Sinks come in a wide selection of materials, so weigh up the advantages and disadvantages before you decide. Go for one with a built-in drainer, but put a dish-rack on it, too – otherwise it is almost impossible to drain more than three or four items. Unless you regularly wash up enormous pans, a deep sink is unnecessary. A fairly small one will be adequate for washing vegetables and ordinary crockery and pots. If space is tight, a sink with a sliding wooden top that doubles as a chopping-board is a sensible purchase.

PLASTIC A budget option. White or pale shades stain very easily, especially with tea or coffee.

STAINLESS STEEL A mid-priced, serviceable and good-looking material. It has to be cleaned often and thoroughly to prevent water marks.

BELFAST AND CERAMIC SINKS More expensive. It is also very easy to break crockery in these sinks. The only cure is to use a plastic washing-up bowl, which spoils the look.

CORIAN This is a man-made material that can be moulded to produce a totally seamless sink and worktop. It's excellent from a hygiene aspect and comes in a range of colours. It's stain-resistant and won't chip your china. On the down side, it's substantially more costly than other options.

RECYCLE THAT WASTE

Whether you cook a great deal or not, a kitchen generates plenty of waste and rubbish, so a decent wastebin is essential. Make the choice between a capacious, smart one, which can be on display all the time, or a smaller one concealed in a cupboard. The smaller type will have to be emptied almost every day.

Try to set aside a space for sorting and recycling your refuse, too. Locate the nearest bottle and can banks, and facilities for recycling different types of paper. If you have a garden, a compost heap will provide all the fertilizer it needs free of charge, while keeping your bins emptier and the environment cleaner.

Redesigning a kitchen is not easy. There are so many aspects to consider and, if mistakes occur, they might have a long-lasting impact. Practicalities have to come first, but this should not stop you achieving the kitchen look you long for. Force yourself to do things in the right order, and you will end up with a room that looks fantastic and cooks fantastic, too.

dining spaces

There are few social activities that carry as much baggage of etiquette and formality as eating. If you have a separate dining room, it is probably the most under-used space in your home. Even though we now take a far more casual approach to mealtimes than previous generations, the dining room in many homes has not shaken off the pre-war atmosphere of a hallowed space with its own particularly restrictive rules.

The quickest and simplest way to erase that sense of a chilly, forgotten room is to knock down a wall and unite your dining room with the rest of your home. This is obviously a serious undertaking which should be approached only with proper forethought and budgeting. Don't even consider a structural change without the guidance of a qualified structural engineer (see Local Law, page 20). If you do embark on a project of this kind, you will probably amalgamate your dining room with either the kitchen or the living area to create one large space. You will doubtless be quite taken aback by the amount of extra room you find, and, with careful planning, you can totally change the way this part of your home functions. Building work takes time, costs money and causes mess and upheaval but, in this instance, the results are certainly worth it.

MAKE IT COMFORTABLE
Your home is for living in, and this applies to each and every part of it. If you have – and opt to keep – a separate dining room, it should be as welcoming and enjoyable as a living room or kitchen, and should be used almost as often, not abandoned for weeks at a time. Its character will be down to the furniture and the way you use the room.

Much of the formality comes from the table and chairs themselves, the crockery and table decoration. Eight gleaming upright chairs around a table-top polished like a mirror is enough to put most people on their best behaviour. Add the best, drop-at-your-peril bone china, intimidating cut-glass goblets and twelve-piece cutlery settings and no one will dare to breathe. Don't aim to recreate an upmarket hotel restaurant in your home. Eating, whether it is a family lunch, Sunday breakfast or dinner for two, should be a pleasure; it's about conversation, laughter, debate and relaxation. These are the elements that will bring a dining room to life.

ADAPT ACCORDINGLY
A well-used dining room has to adapt to a variety of events, and you can create an elegant or totally casual feel simply by the way you dress the table and light the room. A colourful cloth and simple knife, fork and spoon place-settings are all you need for a gathering of friends. Mixed crockery, if your selection is natural and uncontrived, can be very stylish for an informal occasion, but if you are not

Above: In these cabinet doors, where glass is used extensively, be aware that the contents are on display and should look attractive and tidy.

confident about your choices, stick to matching plates. Plain linen, or smart table-mats on a wooden top, plus more cutlery, glasses, and perhaps candles, will create the right background for entertaining business colleagues or acquaintances.

When you do not know your guests well, the less stiff and tense the atmosphere, the more effortlessly the conversation will flow. So put guests at their ease rather than over-awe them with crystal and linen.

SEE SENSE
Flexible lighting is essential to exploit your dining room at all times of day and night (see The Light Stuff, page 46). Different levels of light might be

needed at various stages of an evening meal, especially if you are serving portions at the table before sitting down yourself, so use dimmer switches for overhead lights. People need to be able to see their food, but at the same time the ambience should be mellow. Candlelight is an obvious unbeatable choice for a romantic twosome, and natural daylight is perfect for breakfast or lunch. Remember that other sensations also add to a satisfying dining experience: stimulate the sense of smell with spicy candles and don't forget music as well.

DINING DECOR

Deep, rich reds or greens are the traditional choice for a dining room, and they can look fantastic, especially in the evenings. However, to get the maximum use from your room, consider paler, less heavy colours, too. These will work much better during daylight, and candles can still create the right mood at night. Remember as well that the room should relate to the other spaces around it in mood and colour. A dark, baronial-type dining area is

Below: A good-quality floor paint will withstand heavy wear and tear without requiring varnishing and is an economical way to revitalize shabby floorboards.

likely to be at odds with the rest of your home, and you will not be encouraged to use it if it feels separate and disconnected.

TURN THE TABLES

Predictability is the downfall of many a dining room, and the convention of having a table in the centre, with chairs around it, contributes to unease. It is alien to us to be gathered in the middle of a room, rather than near the sides. Even if you have a small space, try positioning the table at an angle, rather than right at the centre and perfectly parallel to the walls. As with any successful design, a touch of the unexpected can make all the difference.

SEATING PLANS

It might seem like a good idea to buy the largest table your room can accommodate. Having the option of entertaining eight or ten people if you wish is appealing, but a flexible set-up will prove more useful than a huge table. In reality, most of us talk about giving big dinner parties far more often than we actually hold them, so be honest with yourself. If you are going to entertain eight guests only once or twice a year, a table that can extend is the answer. You will then have a comfortable situation for two or four people, with the ability to seat more if required. A circular shape is the best choice for chat because people are close together and the group will not break up into separate discussions. On the other hand, you won't get as much surface area for plates and serving dishes. A rectangular table gives more top space, and conversation will still flourish, provided the table is not too long.

SITTING COMFORTABLY

If you are going to enjoy a leisurely lunch, a delicious dinner or even a speedy breakfast, you must be sitting comfortably. Dining chairs are notoriously hard and some positively discourage lingering at the table. When you are out shopping for them, try out the chairs properly. Sit on one for a good ten minutes. Remember that you will want to lean back between courses and at the end of a meal, and forward to eat, so do move about. You might feel a bit conspicuous making all these movements in a shop, but it is worth it to be able to sit comfortably at mealtimes without becoming either numb or stiff.

As a general guide, metal chairs are cold and hard, and budget café-style ones are rarely pleasant to sit on for any length of time. If you can afford it, go for upholstered furniture, which is far more relaxing. Washable fabric or slip covers are a good investment, but be sure to have a stain treatment in your cupboard to treat spills swiftly. Fabric covers are available for plain wooden chairs, but they have the drawback of turning a linear structure into a solid block. Where space is very tight, stacking or folding chairs make good sense.

Allow yourself some flexibility by keeping four good-looking chairs permanently at the table and another four less expensive folding or stacking chairs in an unobtrusive place. For the few occasions when you are seating more than four, this arrangement will be adequate. Stacking styles are likely to be more comfortable than folding, but will take up more storage space.

UNDER THE TABLE

The floor can strongly influence the personality of a room and should be given as much thought as the colour scheme or furniture. Practicality is always a consideration because no matter how careful you and your guests might be, there will be accidents from time to time. A wooden floor has disadvantages in that chairs will scrape noisily over it

Above: This imaginatively designed glass-topped table, reflecting the colours of the room, and sleek chairs show how style and comfort can go together.

and leave scuff marks on it. It can also seem cold. Create a more intimate impression by adding a soft texture. A rug on a wooden surface works well, as it can be vacuumed and washed or dry-cleaned periodically. Just be sure to use a non-slip backing and be careful not to trip over it when you are carrying hot casseroles or drinks from the kitchen area to the table.

EAT UP

Eating is not just about appeasing hunger. Food and conversation go naturally together and the flavour of one is dulled without the other. Eating is also about stimulating your senses. It should be a complete experience. The solution to a successful dining room, whether you are feeding two or twenty, lies in its atmosphere. Forget formality and protocol and think comfort and conviviality. Enjoy your meal.

space seekers

KITCHEN DINER

the search for space

We sometimes feel we are at the mercy of manufacturers who constantly invent new products we didn't know we needed, when the one thing we really crave is space. We are not just looking for more places to store our clutter, but for room that allows us freedom of movement, clarity of vision and peace of mind. The two go hand in hand – as you put something away you create space.

This lack-of-space situation is often most acute in the kitchen. You might well hanker after metres of worktop, a walk-in fridge, a huge oven and generous dining table, wanting your kitchen to be the magnetic centre of the home with associations of warmth, comfort and activity. But the reality is probably a small space that feels permanently pressurized and more likely to make you tense up than relax.

Preventing possessions from taking over our homes does require some thought, and while you might never be able to afford your dream kitchen, you can review and improve on what you have. You might well be sitting on far more room than you realize, but if it is under-utilized or inconveniently arranged, you cannot get the best out of it. Giving the

DESIGN SOLUTIONS

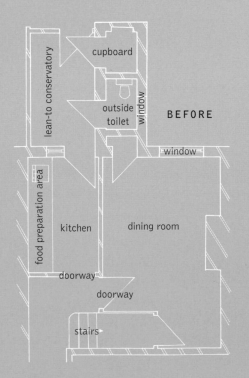

food preparation area | lean-to conservatory | cupboard | outside toilet | window | **BEFORE** | window | kitchen | dining room | doorway | doorway | stairs

This project illustrated a radical space transformation and the value of an outline drawing for pinpointing the potential of the area. This kitchen diner in this Victorian terrace was originally with three floor levels and comprised a small kitchen, a separate dining room with the staircase up one wall and a lean-to conservatory with a corrugated plastic roof attached to an outside toilet.

Having marked the area on paper, a structural engineer confirmed that all internal walls, apart from one tiny section, could be removed, allowing a total rethink of the layout.

The eating area was relocated under a new glass roof, replacing the lean-to and outbuildings. The food preparation area and sink were integrated into a curved worktop with units below. Appliances were fitted alongside extra cupboards under the stairs.

French windows | fold-down wall chairs | table | stool | **AFTER** | window | sink | food preparation area | hob | cooker | stairs | understairs cupboards

impression of room to move is almost as important as what is actually there. Simply reconsidering the style of furniture and the shapes that are dominating a kitchen can vastly increase ease of access and the sense of space around you.

FIND YOUR SPACE

First you need to form an accurate idea of what space you have available. This might sound obvious, but it is surprising how factors such as colour, light and acoustics can influence your impression of size. Kitchens can be especially hard to gauge as there are so many fixed items, such as sinks and fridges, that make it difficult to isolate the framework.

The simplest way to pinpoint how much space you have to play with is to draw a scale plan of your area. For more details on getting this important stage just right, see Picture This, page 9.

DETAILED EXAMINATION

Once you have that all-important clear diagram of the total site, it is time to forget what was there before and really study the 'bones' of your area. Try to see it with a fresh eye, giving every part equal consideration. The dingiest corner could become a stylish spot with the right lighting, decor, flooring and furniture. Seriously consider the potential of forgotten pockets of space, such as under the stairs. With careful planning, and depending on the scale of your staircase, the bulk of your appliances, including fridge-freezer, oven and washing-machine, might fit in there, with some extra space left for storage. Modern units are so well insulated that a fridge-freezer living side by side with an oven will not pose a problem. However, this is not advisable with old appliances.

Study the whole room, which includes looking up and down as well as around. You will find that there is as much scope above your head and under foot as at eye level. For example, shelving for items that you do not need every day can be put up above wall units.

Look beyond the boundaries to what is outside. The view from your room is part of the overall impression, so consider ideas such as sandblasted glass or venetian blinds to mask an ugly vista. If it is attractive, draw attention to it. For instance, paint the window frame in a dark or contrasting colour to isolate the view beyond. You could even consider a glass roof, which will give you the sky as a ceiling – more spectacular and enigmatic than any man-made creation. Simply sensing the wider area outside your four walls will make your room feel larger.

Above left: A wooden table and chairs do not have to match. Inspire interest with a contrast of light and dark surfaces.

Right: With glorious light flooding in through the enlarged French windows and skylights, this eating area destroys the image of the dining room as the darkest, least inspiring room in the house.

Below: An ingeniously designed system of fold-down wall chairs, where individual chairs can be pulled down or slid up out of the way, produces a whole range of different seating combinations.

BREAK DOWN THE BARRIERS

To achieve the most versatile result, it is worth taking a radical step and knocking down some walls to make one large room. If yours is an older property, you might have a separate dining room next to the kitchen which, instead of being reserved for rare 'formal' occasions, can be absorbed into the kitchen by the removal or repositioning of a wall. This might sound ambitious and will certainly involve extra cost and disruption, but you will reap the rewards of your investment. It could totally alter the focus of your kitchen and throw light on to an area you hardly knew was there.

You must seek the advice of a structural engineer before you make any structural alterations and demolish anything (see Local Law, page 20). You will also need to co-ordinate your team,

Left: Thoughtful use of space neatly allows the understairs area to accommodate the oven, dishwasher and fridge as well as additional storage.

Below: The hob splash-back is hinged down one side to give extra storage for crockery.

Right: Hard-wearing and hygienic, a terrazzo worktop can be moulded into a sweeping curve. Choose your own personal combination of background colour and chips.

including a recommended builder and other specialists, such as a plasterer, plumber and electrician. This is definitely not an opportunity for cutting financial corners, so do allow for this kind of expense in your budget (see Desperately Seeking, page 20).

SWEEPING THROUGH

Although you might want to divide your space into 'regions' for, say, cooking, eating and socializing, you do not necessarily need walls to do this. A swathe of kitchen units beneath a curved worktop will naturally form a work area on one side while friends can enjoy a drink on the other and conversation can flow easily between the cook and guests. The units themselves can be standard rectangular ones, arranged in a gentle sweep instead of a straight line. Terrazzo is an ideal choice for a smoothly rounded worktop, as you can give the supplier a

hardboard template from which the exact shape can be moulded.

It is true that a right-angled bank of units would probably give you the same storage and top space, and would be cheaper to install, but wouldn't you feel a bit 'penned in' behind it – cut off from the party? The sense of openness and ease of movement can be killed as easily as it can be captured, so consider as many different arrangements as possible before you finally commit yourself.

CURVED AIR

When space is limited, circles and free-flowing curves are especially comfortable. They soften the ambience of a room and bring a sense of movement, encouraging us to circulate with ease. Unlike straight barriers, which rigidly divide, curves can lead us almost imperceptibly from one area to another. They work well in a kitchen,

Certain styles of furniture will accentuate space, while others will seem to shrink it.

- Avoid solid, chunky pieces. Blocks of anything, including furniture, take up more room visually because you cannot see through or beyond them.
- Furniture mounted on legs allows light to pass below, showing the floor space underneath and further areas of the room. The slimmer the legs, the more space there appears to be around them.
- Translucent materials, and designs with integral gaps, holes or perforations, allow you to see through them and pick up a sense of the room beyond.
- Where there is already a reasonable amount of storage, increase the feeling of spaciousness by not having a base unit where one would normally be. A hob separate from the oven can be installed in a wall-hung worktop supported by slender legs. You will create the look of a fitted piece of furniture, with emptiness all around it, while details of the flooring below and the walls behind will be visible.

where, more than in any other room in the house, you are engaged in practical tasks that require ease of movement between different zones.

USE IT WELL

Many people feel that they do not have enough storage areas in a kitchen. This is often true, but what is also quite common is badly arranged storage. Before you rush into trebling the number of units, ask yourself whether you could use what you have more productively. Pull-out drawers or baskets efficiently fill every last inch right to the back, but still allow you to see all the contents of your cupboard at a glance. Carousels are the only way to utilize a corner unit fully. Don't store your saucepans in a cupboard. This is wasteful and extremely awkward. If you have a handsome set of pans, hang them from hooks on a wall rack; if not, consider investing in some new ones that you can hang up, leaving space in the cupboard for something less attractive. Free up under-the-sink space for items you would rather keep out of sight by choosing a stylish bin that can remain on display.

FLEXIBLE FURNITURE

Think carefully about the furniture you will need. The easiest approach is to envisage what is going to happen in the kitchen, and the pieces you will require. If you have opened up the space to create a kitchen-diner, the table and chairs will be an important consideration. You will probably want a situation where two people could be seated comfortably most of the time, with the option to cater for, say, up to six occasionally. Look for an extending table, and chairs that fold up or stack tidily, and check they are mobile and light enough to move easily into the centre of the room or out of the way. If you choose stacking chairs, be sure you have a place to keep them when they are not in use. The most ingenious furniture is not always found in high streets or catalogues. If you have the chance, investigate the work of students and young designers at exhibitions such as 100% Design or Young Designers and also at local college undergraduate shows. They might well have come up with exactly what you are looking for at a comparable price to the more usual sources.

PICK A COLOUR

There are plenty of colour combinations for kitchens, but if you are planning to eat in this room, too, bear this in mind and opt for something that suits both activities. Shades inspired by the natural world introduce a sense of harmony and

Left: Light pouring through the glass roof accentuates the high-gloss finish of the wood-stained floor.

Below: A huge array of styles of sink is now available. This fan-shaped one fits neatly into the sweeping worktop.

peace, complementing organic forms perfectly. Keep to a family of related tones and you will produce a calm unified effect where no single element will 'jump out'.

Colour is also a useful tool for marking out a specific part of the room, without resorting to physical barriers that would interrupt the openness. For instance, a single wall painted in broad toning stripes will accentuate an area, creating a sense of a separate zone with its own purpose. If you are going for two or more colours, remember that they do not necessarily have to meet at the junction of two walls. Bisecting a flat expanse of wall space with two colours adds to an unconfined atmosphere.

FLOORED!

Floors are so often forgotten, but are one of the largest surfaces in a room and deserve the same attention as walls. A fantastic floor can really define a room. Don't be tempted to use different types of flooring within your space. For maximum impact, opt for just one and make sure it is amazing. Be bold and you will enhance the stature of your room.

A kitchen floor should be non-slip and easy to wipe clean. Wood is an attractive choice that can be teamed with a variety of colour schemes and styles. Remember, you will need to revarnish it every three or four years, which doesn't have to be a lengthy job. Acrylic varnish dries very quickly – you can usually walk on the revarnished floor after an hour. Four or five coats can easily be applied in a day (leaving an hour between each coat).

Don't use the wooden floor simply as a backdrop to everything else in the room. Add some character by mixing different shades of woodstains. These can be painted on to plywood squares which are then laid almost like tiles. You will need seven or eight different tones, and will actually have to work out a regular pattern to achieve a random effect. Test run by making up some painted plywood mini-squares to help you get the combination just right. (See Fab Floors, page 54, for other kitchen flooring ideas.)

JUST AN ILLUSION

Having moved your furniture around or redecorated, you might have experienced the pleasant surprise of finding that your room seems bigger. Much of our perception of a room is really visual trickery, built up around a sense of seeing through or beyond objects, maintaining some true emptiness and using the most inconspicuous ways to define areas with particular functions. In your quest for space, less will definitely give you more.

Above: These elegant lights, suspended in a group around the work area, separate it, almost imperceptibly, from the eating area.

Right: The dominance of glass around the table area gives a feeling of outdoor dining all year round.

slim pickings

NARROW KITCHEN AND DINER

waste not, want not

Even if your diet consists of nothing but convenience food, toast and tea, you need some kind of kitchen. You will want power points for your appliances, worktops to arrange them on, a sink, a fridge, some cupboards for your crockery, and a drawer or two for cutlery and tea towels. And what about a bin and somewhere for cleaning materials? Imagine what you'd need if you wanted to cook in there as well…

We ask a great deal of the kitchen, but it is often a pretty poky space. If you live in a studio flat or tiny home, you might have nothing much more than a passageway with units down one side, so unless it is well designed, with every function and scrap of space carefully considered and accounted for, it can be a complete headache. Living contentedly in a very small property requires a combination of ingenuity and compromise. There are certain facilities, such as a massive range cooker, for example, which are obviously out of the question, however much you long for one. On the other hand, you will be pleasantly surprised at what you can fit in by choosing the right pieces.

DESIGN SOLUTIONS

This property was very narrow – just under 2m (6.5ft)) wide and slightly more than 7m (23ft) long – and was empty. Luckily it was of standard height, which allowed for a second level to be built. The only daylight came from the window in the back corner and a bay window on the front.

The ground floor was divided into cooking, eating and bathing zones. The bathroom was located at the far end for privacy. An opaque glass partition with a sliding door screened it from the other two zones. In such a tiny home, the idea of seeing beyond barriers either by means of slits of holes or by using a transparent material, was vital in maximizing the feeling of space. For the same reason, a contrasting colour on the floor drew the eye the length of the living area.

Curved forms within the cooking and eating zones encouraged maximum freedom of

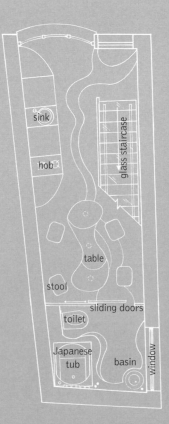

sink

hob

glass staircase

table

stool

sliding doors

toilet

Japanese tub

basin

window

movement and the mobility and flexibility of the furniture made the most of the available space. The table could be expanded and stools on castors doubled as mobile storage. Compromises were made with the choice of a Japanese tub bath rather than the usual full-sized style, and a small-scale hob, dishwasher and sink in the kitchen.

The glass staircase was less than 1m (3¼ft) wide, the minimum size required to meet building regulations. Light passing through its transparent steps and open design made it appear as insubstantial as possible.

The kitchen was fitted into an area just over 2m (6ft) by 2m (6ft) in size. Wall-mounted units provided most of the storage above the appliances. A full-sized oven and fridge were accommodated, alongside a half-size dishwasher, two-ring hob and small sink. Sleek stainless steel was the main material for both appliances and units, bringing uniformity even to a tiny kitchen.

THE RIGHT ANGLES

There is every likelihood that you will feel hemmed in by a narrow space, rather like being in a train carriage, so the choice of base units is crucial. With traditional right-angled cupboards, a partial barrier immediately projects into your already-limited area, reducing freedom of movement. So look for units with gently curving sides instead of square corners. Curves at either end of your run of cupboards and appliances will give the kitchen almost a semi-circular shape, rather than a rectangular one. The loss of storage is minimal, and is more than made up for by the extra floor space and easy circulation encouraged by the flowing contours.

WHEELER-DEALER

Flexibility is one of the keys to successful small-space survival. Unless there is a reason, such as plumbing, for an object to be static, give yourself the option of mobility. For example, a curved corner unit with a worktop can easily be mounted on lockable wheels. Then, if required, it can be rotated to reveal shelving inside. The fact that it has no door to open out from the front gives a smooth line without any protruding handles.

WHAT GIVES?

Even if you have only two or three metres of unit space to play with, it is possible with creative thinking and a little give and take to fit in all the main appliances and plenty of storage. You might not want to compromise on certain appliances, such as a full-sized oven, fridge or washing-machine, but a smaller sink, for example, might not be too much of a sacrifice. Similarly, depending on how much you enjoy cooking, you could consider a mini-hob, with just two rings instead of the usual four, thus freeing up a few valuable extra centimetres for food preparation.

Keep to a simple combination of materials in a restricted area. Too many different surfaces will look muddled. A sleek substance, such as stainless steel, which can be used for splash-backs and eye-level cupboards, is ideal, as it can co-ordinate with a cooker, sink and other appliances. Utilize the walls for cabinets, and remember that you will need one place to store unwieldy items such as a vacuum-cleaner, ironing-board and mop.

Give yourself a single curved floor-to-ceiling unit at one end of the worktop run for this, and fit out the inside with hooks to hang up certain objects rather than just piling everything in and slamming the door. The whole arrangement will be tidier and easier to use and you won't be bombarded with buckets and broom handles whenever you open it.

Above left: Mobile stools that double as storage units make this tiny dining area truly multifunctional.

Right: Even when space is very limited, storage, a food preparation area and appliances can all be accommodated along one wall for convenience and practicality.

WALKING ON GLASS

A dark kitchen is not a pleasure to use. Make the most of any windows by keeping them as unobstructed as possible. If privacy is a problem, go for sandblasted panes, or cover the windows with opaque Perspex, so that daylight will still shine in without your being on view (see Window of Opportunity, page 33). Avoid anything bulky, such as decorative curtains, which take up space, block out light and attract grease and dust.

With some extra effort, you can steal light from another part of your home. If, for instance the room above your kitchen is bright, substitute the usual floorboards for a transparent glass panel, which will give your kitchen a skylight. You will obviously need the right builder for this job. You must also consult a structural engineer and a glazing specialist to ensure that the quality of glass is suitable for flooring, and that it is correctly installed (see The Right Team, page 107). An etched design on the top surface will make the glass non-slip and safe for walking, and also provide an decorative focus when you look up.

A kitchen that is not much more than a corridor is a reality for many people, but it need not spell the end of creative cooking or a splash of style. Be prepared to relinquish certain facilities, and to think laterally about the space you have and how to use it. The result can be good-looking, totally practical and easily equal to any challenge you care to throw at it.

dining spaces

FAST FOOD

The formal dinner party in a grand room kept just for this purpose has virtually died out. Meals nowadays are usually speedy affairs, but you still need somewhere to sit at a table, even for just ten minutes to enjoy a snack. Maybe you think that any sort of dining set-up is not going to fit in. Something, however, can always be done.

ROOM CREATIONS

Wherever space is restricted, the furniture and equipment you decide to install will dictate whether the room functions smoothly or drives you crazy. As you cannot afford to fritter away any space, every piece has to justify its position. In this situation, the more functions an item can perform, the more it will merit inclusion in your design. The look of an object has to take second place to practicality and versatility.

This does not mean that you have to go for a dreary, utilitarian choice every time, but you must give priority to what it will do rather than what it

Left: In a tiny space a mixture of colours will look confusing. Add flair to a simple colour statement using light and dark tones.

Right: No matter how small your room, a striking floor with a snaking band of light-coloured tiles draws the eye into the distance, giving the impression of further space.

looks like. For example, smart collapsible chairs might seem like a good idea, but they will take up valuable room when folded and, apart from providing seating, will not fulfil any other role. Simple cube-shaped cupboards, on the other hand, can have shelves fitted inside, with padded seats on the top and wheels on the bottom. This will give you a box-style stool and a place to store magazines, CDs or videos. In addition, the whole unit is easily moved out of the way, which is especially handy in a very cramped environment where you might need to clear a path for access to another area.

ABLE TABLES

If you are determined to squeeze a substantial item, such as a dining table, into a very confined space, you might need to hunt beyond the usual sources of furniture for something that offers a little bit extra than your average high-street purchase. Specially designed modular pieces, for example, are available for particular circumstances, such as on a narrowboat. A table for two, which can extend to accommodate a family of six, could be your answer. An extra leg can be screwed into the floor to support an additional section of table-top for every pair of diners. Strong magnets secure the table-top to the leg. The screw points for the legs can be laid in a line so that the table expands lengthways to fit the shape of the boat it is intended for.

If your dining area is very limited, there will probably not be much space left to move about, especially when six people are seated, but at least you will have the option of entertaining a group. Like many of the best solutions to small-space situations, there always has to be a degree of compromise.

AROUND THE BLOCK

Remember, the tighter the space available, the more important it is to ensure that what is in it feels comfortable, functions easily and allows for freedom of movement. Avoid hard corners and harsh forms and go for curved shapes. Visualize an oblong table in a very small space. You would feel no inclination to try to manoeuvre around the sharply right-angled edge, but replace the point with a curve and the whole effect is softened and eased.

Shortage of space is obviously going to restrict what you can do in your home, and there is no magical solution. The key to success lies in striking a balance between making the most of what you have and avoiding the impulse to cram in too much. In every instance, think versatility, and make your chosen pieces work very hard for the privilege of being there.

think differently

THE MODERN KITCHEN

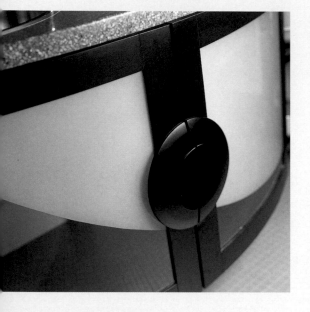

social centre

Apart from the tiniest space with little more than a microwave for heating ready-made meals, the kitchen is now a multi-purpose room. It is where we go to cook, wash up, clean shoes, iron, tend houseplants or look after pets. But more than this, it is the social centre of the home: we congregate there with family and we welcome friends into it to relax and chat while we prepare food for them – not the norm a couple of decades ago. The explosion of interest in cookery and entertaining at home, fuelled by foreign travel and a host of TV programmes and books, means that

the kitchen is often at the heart of our family and social lives, and informality is now the watchword.

higher plane

In a new building, the allotted spot for a kitchen is usually on the ground floor, and chances are that it is rather small. However, above your head you might discover a vast chunk of emptiness which has huge potential. Harnessing this space, particularly in a small property, can revolutionize how you live.

The home has to accommodate you and your needs so, while locating a

DESIGN SOLUTIONS

BEFORE

Like many modern homes, this property had too many rooms, each too small to be useful. The top floor consisted of two tiny rooms separated by a staircase and minute landing. The larger one had a balustrade and was open to the floor below, making it impractical either as study or a bedroom. Windows ran the entire width of this area, so the light and view were amazing.

The mezzanine style of the rooms lent itself to a kitchen, where noise would not be a problem. The spiral stair rose near the centre of the floor, suggesting a natural division between the food preparation and storage and eating zones. As the original kitchen had been located below one end of the mezzanine, plumbing and gas installations were made easier. The curved worktop allowed the flow of movement around the kitchen.

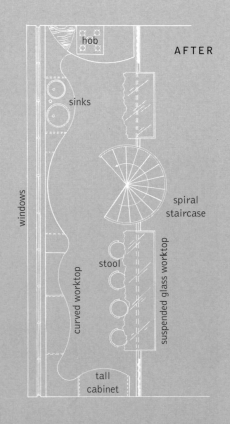

AFTER

kitchen away from the ground floor is still comparatively unusual, it is certainly worth considering. Undertaking a loft conversion or constructing an additional level is a major undertaking, but it can alter the entire focus of a home and prompt you to rethink the traditional layout. A mezzanine (intermediate storey) kitchen, for example, opens up unique possibilities. Situated above a sitting room, it is convenient for socializing without family or guests feeling that the cooking is happening right next to the sofa. It can also offer panoramic views across roofs and treetops, and a bird's-eye view of your own home, as well as bringing in natural light unrestricted by buildings.

The actual size is likely to be substantially larger than your builder originally planned, and if you are feeling particularly greedy, you can even snatch a few more centimetres by

suspending glass worktops from a balustrade overhanging the room below. This is not a DIY task. You will need to find the right builder and specialist glazier to translate your ideas into reality, but the space is there, and if you have the money, why not? (See The Team of Experts, page 20, and The Right Team, page 107.)

Mezzanine floors by nature tend to be long and narrow, but the way to deal with this is to make the elongated shape work to your advantage. Use the separate ends for two independent functions – one for food preparation and cooking, the other for casual eating and storage. The dining part can even double as extra preparation space.

ROUND IT OFF

A typical run of straight units creates a laboratory-like effect, and emphasizes the sensation of sitting in a corridor.

Opt for some curves to soften the angles and avoid leading the eye straight down the entire length of the kitchen. Remember, the floor is one of the biggest surfaces in a room and an innovative treatment can successfully deflect attention from a tunnel-like impression. Use two-toned tiles or vinyl-type flooring to create a large-scale pattern incorporating a bold, swirling effect. As long as the design is simple, it will break up a long stretch of floor space without dominating the area.

Terrazzo, although expensive, is the perfect worktop material in this situation. Available in a colour combination of your choice, it is an update on granite or marble. The large, seamless slabs can be moulded into smoothly rounded forms and, with a hardboard template supplied by your carpenter, your worktop can be custom-made to your specifications. You have the fun of selecting a shade

Above left: A single swathe of sandblasting cuts across a pair of glass doors, concealing unsightly cleaning materials inside.

Right: Angular appliances such as an oven or hob need not interrupt the smooth curves of this kitchen, but can be neatly integrated.

Below: The bread board is designed to slot in perfectly within the shape of the hob surround. Caithness flagstone and terrazzo provide contrast and textural variety.

for the background and for the marble chips to be set into it. Ask to see a polished sample of your colour combination before you proceed.

HANDLE WITH CARE

You can mirror a snaking worktop with softly rounded cupboards below, made from stained or painted wood. These will give a wonderfully rippling form which disguises a boringly straight wall and encourages you to flow easily up and down the length of the room. Be sure to choose handles for these kinds of units with great care. The smooth, undulating line will be utterly destroyed by small, protruding lumps of metal. Take a radical approach and go for something worth grabbing. Large, solid curves can stand really big bold handles, which are almost integral to the design of the doors and drawers. Small, insignificant handles will look like an afterthought.

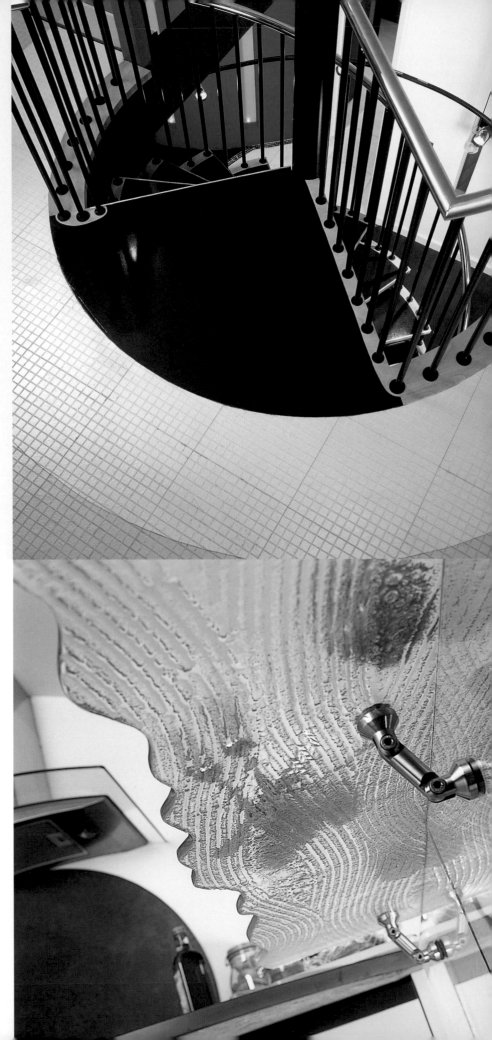

Above right: The spiral staircase indicates the division between the cooking and eating zones.

Right and below: The randomly rippled edges of the glass, reminiscent of frozen liquid, have a natural, uncontrived look. They, too, are completely smooth.

KITCHEN AND DINING SPACES

future furniture

Devote some time to the look of kitchen furniture. Stylish single pieces are now taking over from the traditional fitted kitchen so craved by previous generations. As the purpose of the room alters, so too does the type of unit. There is far less distinction today between a kitchen cabinet for glasses and crockery, and one that could happily hold stereo equipment or decorative pottery by the sofa.

Wood is used increasingly to build beautiful kitchens, which have more in common with handsome furniture than functional units, and you will notice shelves, cupboards and dressers in high-street stores which could just as easily slot into a bedroom, kitchen or living room. To magnify a perception of space, these items are often mounted on legs rather than fitting flush to the floor. This

Right: An enormous curved handle on the dishwasher is as much part of the look as the function. Its stained wood stands out against the sharp green of the dishwasher door and the flagstone worktop above.

TOMORROW'S KITCHEN TODAY

This is where we are heading with kitchen design. Re-visit yours and don't be left behind.

- Kitchens are as much for entertaining and relaxing as cooking. Make yours as inviting as you wish.
- There is no reason to restrict your kitchen to the ground floor. If you have a bigger, brighter space in another part of your home, put your kitchen into it.
- Loosen up! Don't line the walls with rigid units. Introduce fluidity with undulating forms and a mix of materials.
- Explore the very latest in components. Terrazzo, glass, wood and steel are pushing to the fore. Transparency and associations with the natural world are key trends.
- Flexible unfitted furniture, which is not designed just for kitchens, is at the core of contemporary directions.
- Free-standing furniture can be made mobile by attaching castors to them. The units can then be moved out of the way when not needed, particularly useful where space is tight.

Above: A single, bold semi-circular shape breaks into three sections to form chunky drawer handles.

immediately reinforces the impression of a piece of furniture, rather than something built in, makes it seem larger and also gives you that all-important chance to see the ground beneath or wall beyond.

Materials for kitchens are evolving, too. In the techno-rush of modern life, natural substances are assuming great importance, reminding us of our roots and helping us to feel more secure. Wood, waxed or polished to show its inherent beauty, is growing ever more popular, as are stone-like floorings and worktops. Painted and plastic finishes are giving way to steel, slate and glass.

MASTER GLASS

Glass is one of the most exciting materials you can use in a kitchen. If the idea conjures up images of a frosted square in a cupboard door, or perhaps heat-resistant 'oven to tableware', you should really investigate this substance.

In the past few years technology has advanced immeasurably and glass today has enormous potential.

On a practical level, its smooth, flat surface makes for almost effortless cleaning, so it is extremely hygienic for worktops and food preparation areas. It can also be made incredibly tough, so it is absolutely safe, with no danger of shattering or cracking. Glass can be moulded to form decorative surfaces or curved to make a cooker-hood or cupboard door. Sandblasting individualizes each panel, creating patterned or opaque areas that can screen pipework or the inevitable dish-cloths and cleaners under the sink. As a substance, glass embodies the idea of transparency, which can segregate a space in an almost imperceptible way. It has a quality of freshness and class, without seeming ostentatious.

Specialized glass products are not yet in the mass market, but they are

Above: The facility to raise and lower this tap means it doesn't protrude or obstruct unnecessarily when not in use.

becoming more widely available as the presence of glass in modern design is growing. It is comparable in price with granite, so it is not a budget choice, but if you are looking for a kitchen with a truly forward-thinking style, this is your answer. The first step is to find a company that is experienced in commercial structural work with glass. Do not be tempted to pop into the local glazier's. To go beyond the norm and exploit this beautiful substance, you must approach the experts and be prepared to spend some money (see The Right Team, page 107).

Left: Flowing curves disguise the long, slim shape of this kitchen and ease traffic between the different zones.

Right: The suspended glass breakfast-bar gives an impression of eating off a floating plate while being seated in mid-air, and provides extra space for either food preparation or snacking. Small glass upstands prevent anything dropping to the floor below. A huge, glass-fronted cabinet is the modern replacement for the traditional kitchen dresser.

bedroom spaces

One factor sets the bedroom apart from every other location in your home. While friends or family might wander around your living room, sit and chat in the kitchen, use your bathroom and even pop their heads into your office, the bedroom is different – the only really private room, from where everyone but a partner is excluded.

With this in mind, you would expect the bedroom to be a really special sanctuary, a place of utter self-indulgence. Strangely, the opposite is more often the case. Research shows that bedrooms come way down our list of decorating priorities, behind kitchens, living rooms and bathrooms. This room is not on display, so we tend to make do, not really bother too much because no one sees this particular environment. No one except you, that is. Extraordinary to think that in the place you retreat to for rest, recuperation and the recharging of your batteries, you could be sleeping on a lumpy mattress, surrounded by colours you dislike, reading in poor light, or straining to watch a badly positioned TV. If this is the case, it is time to think about yourself and make your bedroom a personal heaven.

SLEEPING SHADES

Not only do you go to sleep in the bedroom, you wake up there, so the different functions and atmospheres of the room have to be tailored to suit both ends of the day. As a general rule, busy patterns and very bright colours are best avoided. Even though you might not be aware of it, both are mentally stimulating and will not encourage you to drift off to sleep, or wake up gently. If you adore vibrant shades and have your heart set on a shocking pink or fiery orange bedroom, go halfway by using this just on the wall behind your head. Paint the rest of the room in a softer, paler tone. Then, when you are standing in the room, you will have a strong impression of colour, but will not be dazzled by it

when you are lying half-asleep in bed. Peaceful greys and blues, or warm pinks, creams and yellows are all appealing. Bold reds and purples are not very restful, and certain greens have slightly institutional overtones that you might prefer not to wake up to.

HOLD BACK THE LIGHT

Bedroom windows can be treated in various ways, and the choice depends on personal preference. Do you like to be woken gradually by daylight filtering in, or do you prefer to remain cocooned in pitch darkness for as long as possible? If you decide on curtains, stick to a plain fabric, or a simple tonal pattern. 'Dress' curtains – drapes that frame the window, but don't actually draw – are an alternative. Blinds can be pulled down for privacy.

TOUCH OF LUXURY

Bed linen, wall and window treatments, flooring and furniture all inject colour into your design; and its instant visual impact usually makes colour our first point of contact. But in the bedroom, where lights are often low, the sense of touch can come to the fore. Treat your skin to some luxurious fabrics, such as silk, velvet or fake fur. If a glorious bedspread is beyond your pocket, buy or make some gorgeous cushions to bring a touch of opulence to plain bedding. Surround yourself with fabrics you want to snuggle up to. If your dressing-gown is still the same sensible one you had for Christmas ten years ago, you can't hope to feel pampered or special. Indulge in one that enfolds you in sensual softness. It is all part of your private bedroom experience.

BARE YOUR SOLES

A bedroom should be about total physical comfort, so bare feet will probably be the norm. A wooden floor is surprisingly chilly, and can be noisy, while coir matting is very harsh to walk on. Carpet is really the only option for comfort and warmth under foot.

Above: A well-positioned reading light is essential for every bed. Here, the light is fixed to a side panel at right angles to the headboard.

As it will receive less wear than in other parts of the home, the carpet can have a slightly longer pile, a fancy weave or a textured finish. A lighter shade is also possible, but do be practical. You will still have heavy traffic areas around the bed. A rug can help to minimize the wear.

SERENE SCENE

Stimulate your sense of smell, too. Scents are very powerful and can evoke all kinds of atmospheres and responses. Aromatherapy candles or oils can help you unwind at night, or energize you in the morning. If you enjoy these in the bath, then just extend the pleasure into the bedroom. Fresh flowers also have a place. It might seem like an extravagance, but that is what this space is all about, and there is no harm in treating yourself from time to time. A single flowering orchid in a pot will look beautiful for two or three months and will not set you back as much as a weekly bouquet. There are also plenty of low-maintenance foliage plants that can bring life and freshness to any room. At all costs, avoid bringing anything into the bedroom that detracts from the atmosphere of relaxation and peace. This goes particularly for laundry, which, festooned over the radiator, will ruin any semblance of serenity. Keep it in a utility area.

Your bed and mattress (see page 85) are two of the most important purchases you can make.

Remember, you will be spending about a third of your life on these, so don't skimp or buy in a hurry.

ALL IN A BOX

Has it ever struck you as odd that you can go to the same shop for a 'fitted bedroom' as you can for a kitchen? The two rooms could hardly be further apart in style, function and feeling, so how come they are presented together like this? The concept of the fitted bedroom has really come about from kitchen manufacturers' desire to create two business opportunities by adding different finishes to the same basic products. However, if you are hoping to bring any sort of individuality or character to a bedroom, this does not really work. With a kitchen, you add extras such as a table and chairs, tiles, worktops, decoration and maybe other furniture, too. Once a fitted bedroom is in place, there is little scope to add anything apart from carpet, curtains and bedding. Fitted wardrobes might well make the best use of available space, and could be the right choice, but the rest of your furniture does not need to match them.

To break the mould, first clear your mind of any preconception about bedroom layout. Go back to basics, with a scale drawing of your space (see Picture This, page 9), and really look at what you have. For example, the bed does not have to go exactly in the middle of a wall. Experiment by positioning it off-centre, or at an angle, or even under a window if it is not too draughty. Wardrobes work well in alcoves, but check other locations, too, before you make up your mind. Sometimes there is not the space to play with and your options might be limited, but pause for thought and don't automatically choose the most obvious arrangement.

MATCHING BATCH

Matching sets of furniture are another bedroom phenomenon that can be adopted unthinkingly.

CROWDED OUT

As in every room in your home, space is likely to be something you would love a bit more of in your bedroom. Since no outsiders see this room, 'clutter-spots' can develop without your realizing. Watch out for the following:

- Trunk or chest at the end of the bed. Use this to store spare bedding and blankets, which you need from time to time, not heaps of old magazines that you never look at.
- Back of the door. Remember, one hanging item can rapidly become half a dozen, and then it is impossible to get at any of them. No matter how pretty your dressing-gown is, hang it on a hook inside a wardrobe or somewhere out of sight. Don't litter your view from the bed.
- Top of the wardrobe. All kinds of articles can get shoved up here and just forgotten. Clear them out periodically, and get rid of any that you have not used for two years. This space is precious, so don't fill it with unwanted items.
- Bedside cabinets. These are another easy place to shut things away and forget about them. A table rather than a cabinet will discourage hoarding, and the smaller it is, the less likely it will be to accumulate anything other than essentials.
- If space is really tight, you could take a tip from New York apartment dwellers. In that city, where square metres are like gold-dust, it is common practice to rent a self-storage unit and keep out-of-season clothing or infrequently used cumbersome ski equipment outside the home. This might sound extreme, but it could be the answer to your storage problems, and the monthly outlay would be fairly modest.

They can include everything from the bed itself, to wardrobes, chests of drawers, dressing-tables and bedside furniture. The effect is static, predictable and completely dull. These kinds of suites – when the bed is in the centre of the room, flanked by twin cabinets or tables, a pair of identical lamps and a matching wardrobe for each partner – also promote the idea of unbending symmetry.

You will achieve a looser, more relaxed feel with individual items, which harmonize without being alike in style and finish. The actual furniture can still be of the same size and capacity as the matching pieces, but a mix of polished or varnished woods with painted or Melamine-type surfaces makes a much more personal, less 'off-the-shelf' impact.

USER-FRIENDLY

We think of the bedroom primarily as a place for sleeping, but we actually expect it to perform several other functions, too. It is here that you will most

likely dress for work, apply make-up or style your hair. You might also use it for practical tasks, such as sewing or ironing. You will change and freshen up here before an evening out, or spend a relaxed night in, curled up watching TV or reading.

Lighting is key to a range of different activities, both in practical terms and in creating the right atmosphere (see The Light Stuff, page 46). Flexibility is all-important, so make sure you have a well-positioned lamp for reading or close work, a low-level glow for watching television and a main light for activities such as ironing or vacuuming. Don't forget candles for a romantic mood, but be sure they are placed on a heat-proof surface, well away from flammable materials.

RIGHT REFLECTIONS

For most people, the bedroom doubles as a dressing-room, so the location of mirrors is an important consideration. To make the best of your appearance, you must be able to see yourself from head to foot, so a full-length mirror is something you should not be without.

For make-up and hairstyling, a dressing-table set-up is ideal. It gives you a place to keep cosmetics, toiletries and hair accessories, and, with a phone and diary to hand, can work as a small desk. If possible, it should be placed in front of a window to make full use of natural light and you need to make provision for good artificial lighting in the evening. Make sure you have a decent-sized mirror here so that you can see exactly what you are doing, and a power point in the right place for your hairdryer. You might find that the best position for your mirror means that you keep catching sight of your reflection when you're in bed. Consider a swivel or tilting mirror if this is annoying.

Left: These fabric-covered storage boxes look smart and well thought out as opposed to cardboard ones, which can give a functional, temporary feel.

GOOD VIEW

Snuggling under the duvet, watching an absorbing film on television, is one of life's pleasures and the correct positioning of your set is crucial. If you can't see it comfortably without straining either your eyes or your neck, it will not be relaxing. Bedroom TVs are often too large for the space and not positioned far enough away. Wall brackets are ugly and often fixed too high up, so you are permanently tilting your head. If you can, buy a portable set and place it either on a trunk or a unit at the foot of your bed. Height-wise the screen should be at eye level when you are sitting up to watch. A stand or table on wheels is worth considering so that the TV can be pushed against a wall when it is not in use.

double spacing

Wardrobe space is perennially in short supply, but you might have more than you think: it could just need reorganizing. The usual situation is a single rail, the width of your cupboard, with about 2m (6ft) below. Unless you live in ankle-length dresses and coats, a large proportion of your clothes will require only half-length hanging space. Two rails – one below the other – with a sufficient gap between for your longest shirt or folded trousers will double the capacity. Canvas compartments that hang from a rail inside the wardrobe are useful as a temporary substitute for a more efficient arrangement.

A PLACE FOR EVERYTHING

Whatever space you have, think before you decide what should go there. Clothes and accessories that come out only a few times a year should be stored in the least accessible spots, leaving everyday articles to hand. Use the bottom of the wardrobe for shoes, but keep them in pairs on a shoe-rack, not in a disorganized heap. Store less-frequently used items, such as

suitcases, at the top, and remember that you can put hats, rucksacks or handbags inside them. It is helpful to attach labels so that you know what each contains without having to pull everything down.

If you have drawers in your bed base, make use of them. If you simply have space under the bed, buy plastic boxes on wheels (from DIY stores) and slide them underneath. Transparent ones with lids are a good choice, as you can see everything inside and the contents won't get dusty. Under-bed drawers are another convenient place to store shoes or items, such as belts, scarves and gloves, that are not needed every day.

PUT ON A FRONT

Once you have organized the inside of the wardrobe, don't forget that the outside can be inexpensively revamped, too. Even if you think it looks particularly tatty, the basic carcass is probably fine. Simple touches, such as a coat of paint and new, up-to-the-minute handles, could make all the difference. Alternatively, dress the doors in fabric or cover them with a real wood veneer.

all yours

In today's world, so much is expected from each person. We push ourselves ever harder and relax less and less. A bedroom should be a sanctuary from modern life, a room which is just yours, secluded from friends or family. It is where you can feel utterly peaceful, where you can simply be yourself.

Left: Its sheer size makes the bed the dominant feature in a bedroom. This can be enhanced by an unusual headboard. Positioning the bed away from a wall also draws attention to it.

relax with style

pleasing prospects

Above: The similar colours of the wall panel, vase and poppy seedheads highlight the overall scheme.

Bedrooms are special places in a home – ultimate personal sanctuaries, where it is essential to feel totally at ease. Faced with the box-like space that often passes for the 'master-bedroom', however, you might be unsure how to engender that ideal combination of serenity and modernity.

Textures are a vital, but often over-looked, factor in making a bedroom both comfortable and stimulating. Visual and sensual experience comes from having a variety of surfaces. The idea of satin sheets, for example, might not immediately appeal to you, but in a shimmering shade of pearl grey, they create a subtle, beautiful surface and a perfect foil for a soft tangerine checked blanket and ribbed velvet upholstery.

A further dimension can be added by considering large expanses, such as walls. Mixing panels of wood and fabric, for example, will create an embossed effect on a flat vertical plane. Or you can use plywood to create an undulating wall and highlight its wavy form by adding a covering of fake suede. You can then use the curves in the wall as an exhibition space. For instance, a pair of tall, strikingly twisted shelf units in pale wood will glow against a velvety backdrop, illuminated from above by neat halogen spots (see Sources Made Simple, page 48).

DESIGN SOLUTIONS

BEFORE

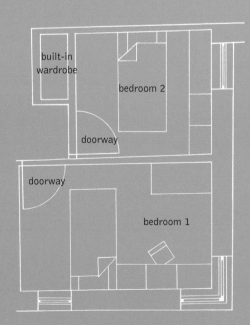

built-in wardrobe

bedroom 2

doorway

doorway

bedroom 1

This project changed two cramped bedrooms and a poky bathroom (see page 128) into a relaxing double bedroom and *en suite* bathroom. All internal walls and a built-in wardrobe were removed to reveal the basic shape. Three doorways became a single entrance so that sleeping and bathing zones of almost equal importance could be created within one space, divided by a change of flooring. A conventional wall was replaced by a curved one of opaque glass bricks, giving equal structural support, but allowing light through from the hall. An undulating wall between this bedroom and the one next door created storage alcoves and a decorative feature on either side.

Positioning the bed at an angle focused attention on it. Repetition of simple cylindrical and square forms throughout created unity.

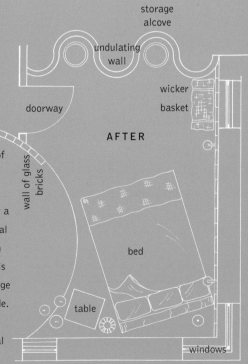

storage alcove

undulating wall

doorway

wicker basket

AFTER

wall of glass bricks

bed

table

windows

SURPRISE YOURSELF

A design scheme should always contain one unexpected element, whether a startling splash of colour or the presence of an unexpected shape or material. This sharpens the overall effect and safeguards the result from seeming rigid or contrived. Think of your bed as a mobile piece of furniture. By positioning it at an angle, rather than centre to the wall, you will change the whole focus and feel of the room. An angled bed frees up space and increases the flow of movement around the room.

BED AND BOARD

The bed is naturally the key piece of furniture in a bedroom, but we are inclined to view it as a boring necessity rather than an important object that merits special attention and investment. We make the same one last for years and spend more time choosing a sofa or table than shopping for a bed.

It is, though, worth budgeting for a good-quality bed and the best mattress you can afford. In general, a mattress should be changed every six or seven years; a good frame should last longer. When you are looking at beds in the shop, test out the various choices by lying on them for at least ten to fifteen minutes. Make a point of turning over, moving around and sitting up as if reading a magazine or watching television. If there are two of you, try it out together – within limits, of course! A comfy bed is essential. If you cannot sleep well, you cannot function properly during the day, so take care to make the right choice for you.

Many of the bed frames currently available are wooden or wrought iron, and while these do look stylish, they are not exactly soft and yielding on your back if you want to sit up to enjoy your favourite programme or read a book. You could get by with lots of large pillows, but a padded headboard is the solution. If a scallop-edged, plush-covered 1970s relic springs to mind, don't panic! Good-looking contemporary fabrics are available. If you can't find what you are looking for, you could make a simple padded slip-on cover for your existing headboard. Alternatively, ask a curtain-maker or upholsterer to make a padded headboard to your design and specifications.

SISTER SHAPES

An overall design can be said to be working when the different elements seem to be at ease with each other, neither too rigidly matching and predictable, nor bewilderingly unconnected. If you have gone for the clean, unfussy lines of a simple chunky bed and square or rectangular forms, a few of one contrasting shape, such as a cylinder, will loosen and enliven the

Right: Tall, twisting shelves have been chosen for their dramatic presence, not their practicality. Against an undulating background of fake suede and lit from above by halogen spots, they give a feast of textural interest and shadows.

Below: Even the simplest cream-coloured window blind can add another layer of detail to a design. The woven look is in keeping with the square panels on the walls, and texture is the focus of this room.

general impression. A cylinder, like a cube, is a plain geometric shape, but its rounded form will offset sharp corners and straight lines. A cluster of three huge, floor-standing candles of varying heights and colours will form a curving sculptural shape that contrasts beautifully with a cube-shaped bedside table. A mesh-like pattern of squares on the wall will be brought into focus by opaque glass tubular light fittings suspended lantern-style in front.

WELL CONNECTED

In newly built homes, and some old ones, the main bedroom might have a private bathroom attached. The latest approach to the 'master-bedroom with en suite facilities' is to open up the total area so that the two functions – sleeping and bathing – are within one room. To achieve this, do not put up a dividing wall: just use a simple change of flooring, say, tiles in the bathroom,

timber in the bedroom. In this way, the two parts are distinct but fully connected and you can see the entire area from any point in the room.

A change of flooring from light tiles to dark wood will also create distinct differences in each space. The light flooring will seem fresh and calm, while a dark bamboo floor will bring a sense of warmth and security. Available in large strips, bamboo is a wonderfully versatile material as it can be stained any colour. With the deepest stain it is virtually indistinguishable from endangered hardwoods, such as mahogany or teak. Rich, deep brown polished woods are taking over again from pale, blond woods, so you can achieve an up-to-date look without damaging the environment.

MIRROR IMAGE

An effective design technique is to take a distinctive feature from one zone and

mimic it in another, thus reinforcing the concept of two halves of a whole. This can be achieved by something as simple as a colour that appears in both places, or a more complex idea. A wall of opaque glass bricks in the bathroom, for example, can be echoed on the bedroom wall with fake-suede squares in pale green, framed by dark-stained wood panels. The twin patterns of regular rows will mirror and balance each other and unify the whole.

SLEEP WELL

Bedrooms are about switching off from daily stresses and the outside world. They need to be havens of tranquillity and places where, surrounded by a restful harmonious atmosphere and comfortable furnishings, you can totally relax before tackling the next day's challenges. A place where you will feel better at night as well as in the morning.

Left: Designed by a recent graduate, the beautiful torso doubles as a storage unit and gives a focal point to the bed and room.

Right: A neat, blond wood bracket fixed against a dark-stained panel sets off this simple tubular glass light. The cylindrical form is in keeping with the straight lines on the wall behind.

Below: An adventurous combination of surfaces, such as satin and ribbed velvet, seems both indulgently luxurious and totally contemporary.

practical style

TEENAGE BEDROOM

Above: With two or more beds, complementary rather than matching bedding looks effective.

work, rest and play

Although perhaps separated by only five years, it is almost impossible to credit that a scrawny twelve-year-old obsessed with boy bands or computer games and a poised young adult embarking on college or a career are one and the same person. Youngsters change rapidly during their adolescent years and are notoriously difficult to please. A teenager's bedroom is a real challenge.

A room for this age-group must fulfil several functions, which need to be given equal priority when you are at the planning stage. Obviously, the bedroom is primarily for sleeping in. Second, your child needs somewhere quiet and prop-erly equipped for homework. Third, you cannot escape the fact that he or she will want to have friends in, often to stay over, listening to music, fooling around with make-up, playing portable computer games or just lounging about. It is important for youngsters' self-esteem and growing independence that they have somewhere to go with their mates, away from the family, so this must also be addressed.

All these requirements have probably set you thinking that your child needs the largest room in the house, but everything can be accommodated in a fairly small, stylish and appealing space. Remember, teenagers are incredibly fussy.

BEFORE

AFTER

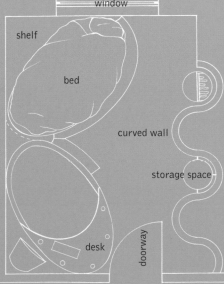

DESIGN SOLUTIONS

In some respects this small bedroom had to perform as a mini-apartment. Space was needed for a bed, study area and storage, and also for friends to stay over. The original design had a built-in wardrobe jutting into the hall, creating a recessed entrance to the room. The doorway was pushed out in line with the back of the wardrobe, which could then be removed and the area incorporated into the main space. Storage was created in the natural alcoves of the curving wall shared with the main bedroom next door.

It was important to produce the effect of two separate zones for study and sleeping, so ovals were used to mark out each area. The study was located on a raised platform, lit from below, to add a sense of a designated working area. Below the oval bed, a pull-out mattress could accommodate overnight stays. In each instance, the rounded edge created a corner shelf, which made an ideal bedside storage spot or computer station.

Ideally, you would hope, the design of a teenager's room will last a good five years. But as fads and phases are part of growing up, this can be a problem. At certain stages, a 'themed' bedroom might seem like a dream come true. But whether it is football, pop groups, cartoons or dolls, be cautious of going all out for this kind of décor. Your son or daughter might adore it for a year or so, but then it could become a source of embarrassment with friends, and give rise to anguished pleas for a new look. The best solution is to find a compromise, perhaps using stencils which can be painted over easily, and affordable accessories, which will not make too much of a hole in your purse when changed.

UP TO BED

Curving contours are an excellent way of bringing life and a sense of movement to a space of any size, and they also serve to delineate different functions without physically dividing the room. Raised areas also add interest and give a sense of separate zones. In a rectangular room, two oval platforms, for example, can be used to mark out areas for a bed and a desk. Where the rounded edge of the bed meets the wall, it will form a boxed-in corner. Use the top ledge for a clock, radio, lamp and stereo. Wiring and power points can be neatly concealed inside the box. If the room is not large enough for seating, youngsters will happily lie around on the bed, but make it comfy with plenty of cushions. Beanbags are also a good option because they take up less space than chairs and can be stacked up or stored fairly tidily when not needed.

ONE-NIGHT STAND

Provided there is sufficient floor space, you can create a pull-out bed, similar to a large drawer, which fits under the main one. It need not be much more than a foam mattress. This will give your son or daughter somewhere for friends to stay the night, but they will not be so comfortable that they will never want to go home. Teenagers rarely keep their beds tidy or open their curtains every day, so there is no point in trying to achieve the impossible. Instead of pure white cotton bedding, go for easy-care fabrics that will look reasonable with just a bit of a shake, and put up Venetian or roller blinds.

OLE BLUE JEANS

Provided there is some carpeted floor space or a rug for sprawling on, a single sofa should fulfil a teenager's seating requirements. An old sofa can be individualized and revitalized by a loose cover, which also has the advantage of being washable.

Right: A second bed is easily moved out from beneath this custom-made oval bed, providing a crash-pad for friends.

Below: Radios and stereos are inevitable, so make provision for these. A boxed-in ledge or simple bedside shelf will keep everything tidy.

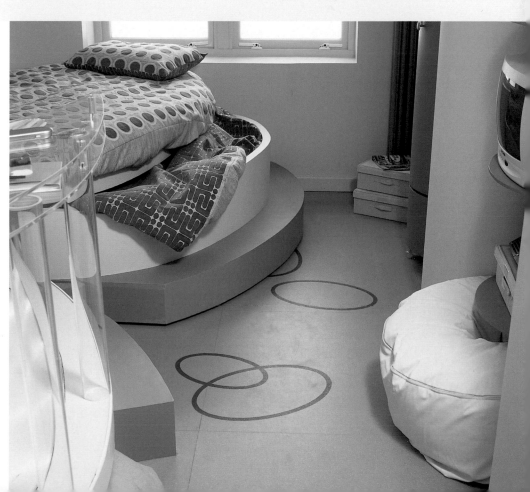

Obviously, a dark shade is practical, but why not think beyond the plain, off-the-shelf options, which are unlikely to inspire the recipient? Every kid wears jeans, so denim is a totally acceptable look, as well as a fantastically hard-wearing fabric. Raid your local charity shop for as many jeans, jackets and other denim items as you can lay your hands on, and join them together into one large piece of cloth. This can then be made into a loose cover or used as a throw for the sofa. A heap of denim-covered cushions will also be well received.

RAISING THE STAKES

As these years are some of the most important for education and exams, anything that encourages studying has to be good. A desk is essential and, doubtless, a computer too. An atmosphere of order and efficiency will help concentration, but the surroundings will also need to be as appealing as possible. If they like the style, children will want to sit in there more often.

A specific place in the bedroom for study – perhaps a raised area – will help put a teenager in the right frame of mind for schoolwork. As less headroom is needed for sitting at a desk, a platform, with some storage space below, can be built even under a sloping ceiling. A change of flooring will also add to the impression of entering a different sphere with another function. A semi-opaque floor, made from Perspex or the latest substance, Prismex, can be installed on a raised base, and subtly lit from below. It looks so stunning that your student will be itching to get up there.

Having been used commercially for years, Perspex is now infiltrating the home and is a fantastic material for a teenager's room. A Perspex desk, with a half moon shaped top, has just the right amount of novelty, style and futuristic feel to appeal to youngsters. A carpenter could supply a hardboard template from which the desk top could be cut. Don't attempt this yourself – find a company that is experienced in working with Perspex. A double-layered top allows for a neat storage shelf under the main working surface so that stationery and papers can be clearly seen. Perspex tubes can be used for the legs. The addition of a see-through chair to this work-station should raise a glimmer of enthusiasm from even the most non-committal young person.

Alternatively, employ a carpenter to build something chunky, off-beat and unexpectedly colourful, and as far from a school desk as he can make it. It can also be made uniquely personal by

incorporating your child's initials into the design and can cost less than you might expect.

The right environment and accessories can go a long way towards inspiring a positive attitude to home-work and studying. Even simple, inexpensive touches, such as smart, fashionable stationery and colourful files, can help.

WALL ORDER

Posters can be the bane of a parent's life, but at some stage most teenagers plaster the walls with them. If the collection is really getting out of hand, and some are tatty or faded, try to reach a compromise. You could suggest making a montage of favourites, or buying two or three reasonable frames to set off the best ones, but don't waste too much energy on this – your teenager will outgrow them quite quickly.

MAKING CONNECTIONS

It is vital for a room to grow with its occupant. When you are at the planning stage, make sure you allow for sufficient power points, bearing in mind the ever-increasing quantity of appliances that will be required. Boys and girls will both have a computer, CD player, stereo, TV and hairdryer, or even a tropical fish tank, and a daughter might have a styling brush or facial steamer on top of all that. As the Internet is already an accepted part of education, your child will need his or her own access to a separate telephone line with a handset, although not necessarily a new number. It is far safer to install extra facilities than risk overloaded plugs and dangerous extension flexes. For everyone's sanity, think about sound insulation, too. It is heartless to treat teenagers to a new stereo or an electric guitar and then expect them to be quiet.

UNDER-EIGHTEEN RULES

- Spark interest with unusual shapes and materials, which will encourage a teenager to use a desk, cupboard or whatever.
- Give yourself a break. Insist on easy-care textiles, wipe-clean flooring and sufficient sound-proofing.
- Try to accommodate the things that are important to them, such as a place for friends to stop over, their computer and Internet access.
- Accept that they will grow out of certain aspects of their room fairly quickly and try to steer them away from decisions they might regret, such as obscure colours or strong themes.

Left: Perspex brings a light, stylish and futuristic feel to the work-zone. Spare sockets and an extra phoneline won't go amiss.

Right: An undulating wall lifts a mundane style of room. The curves supply storage space and interlocking ovals on the floor reflect the theme.

Below: Circular shelves slot into a curved wall and give more surface space than conventional rectangular ones.

SOUND STEREOS

Unless your taste in music is the same, it is probably best for your teenager to have their own stereo or CD player so that they can enjoy their personal favourites without disturbing the rest of the family. This does not need an elaborate shelving arrangement: it can sit quite happily on the floor where it is easily accessible.

A plain, painted MDF box can be used to surround and protect the stereo from knocks and spills, and a simple circular frame, with a flat edge that sits on the floor, can be attached to the front. Rather than being just a black cube unrelated to anything, it will give the equipment a bit more presence and keep trailing wires a little more under control.

Teenagers also tend to have piles of CDs, which can get very messy if they are just stacked on a shelf. Matching the hi-fi box storage in the form of

wall-mounted MDF boxes, framed and painted, will keep things tidy and also create a visual statement of colour and shape. This sort of storage is economical and easy to make, so who knows, your teenager might even construct it himself.

KEEP IT CLEAN

Wherever one or more teenagers gather, drinks, food and cosmetics will be dropped, and no matter which type of carpet is under foot, it will become grubby and stained. Practicality is the major consideration in a young adult's room, and a wipe-clean surface is the only answer. Girls will appreciate the softness and warmth of a rug under foot, but choose a washable one. Easy-to-wipe-clean does not condemn your offspring to dreary rubber flooring. There are plenty of stylish and interesting choices around. Look for unusual surface details such as subtle sparkles

and modern geometric patterns.

Clothes, even if they seem to spend most of their time on the floor, need somewhere to hang. An imaginatively planned wardrobe might encourage more tidiness than all the reminders in the world, so if the opportunity arises, opt for something a little out of the ordinary. An undulating wall (see plan, page 88), for example, will produce tube-shaped alcoves that can

Left: A comfortable, supportive chair and a roomy desk at the right height are essentials, regardless of the age of the student. An unconventional design and colour might even make homework more appealing!

Above right: A punchy, eye-catching effect is achieved by creating a series of small storage units rather than a single one.

Right: Sleeping space for three is concealed under the raised platform. When the beds are stored, they do not take up any floor space.

Far right: Denim and camouflage reflect a teenage boy's taste and are likely to be well received.

be fitted out with hanging space and doors, or with a column of circular shelves to take a television and storage boxes.

KEEP IT COOL

A neutral palette of greys, taupes, khakis and creams might not instantly spring to mind, but they are the best unisex choices for teenagers. They work really well with geometric patterns, giving an almost technological feel, and look smart, chic and moody, which is satisfying for fifteen-year-olds, who often want absolutely everything in black. Try to anchor a design around something you have seen them choose for themselves – a pattern, such as a check or a print that they are happy to wear on a T-shirt, or a classic fabric such as denim, can be the springboard for your scheme. A teenage boy lives in horror of anything 'girly', so subdued colours

are a good bet, but don't let the overall effect become too dark. Remember that adolescents are often very moody by nature. Look for something that gives you a clutch of related tones, some deeper, some paler, so that you can team bed linen and other accessories to fit in. For girls, the main alternative is a strong combination of purples and cerises, which feels both feminine and sophisticated.

Teenagers are not always easy to live with. Sometimes they know only what they hate, and can't actually express what they like. They need support and encouragement to study throughout their school years, and space to be themselves, to let off steam, and be with their friends. Often they just need some time alone.

However tough it gets, just remember a teenager-friendly environment will help – and there is life after the teenage years.

GOING TO PIECES

Flooring for teenagers – who are not renowned for their fastidious or dainty natures – has to be practical. Food, coffee and sticky canned drinks will inevitably be spilled, so an easy-to-clean surface is essential. There are lots of choices, from wood to all kinds of plastic and rubber materials.

Carpet is really not suitable, but something reasonably soft under foot will make the seating and socializing area more comfortable: carpet tiles are a sensible and reasonably priced compromise for the following reasons.

- More often used in offices and commercial premises, they are very durable and stain-resistant, as spills tend not to be absorbed. The beauty is that you can lift out grubby individual squares, clean them and then replace them.
- With a little time and effort, you can create a jigsaw-type effect by combining several colours cut and fitted together into any shape of your choice. Boys will appreciate a masculine design, such as camouflage, while girls might go for a bold daisy or star shape.
- Your choice of colours from the wide range available will also add to the male or female appeal. In this way you can create an eye-catching focus and separate the seating zone from the rest of the room.

BED-CRED

A bed with a simple, utilitarian, masculine edge can be made very inexpensively from two large sheets of MDF for the base, which is then painted and set on to chunky, industrial-looking, lockable castors. A painted headboard with a cut-out detail will complete the job. Mobility is essential to free up space for a range of other purposes. For example, when your son wants three of his friends to stay over and sleep on the floor, the main bed can be pushed to one side.

Left: Paint a sloping ceiling the same colour as the wall, otherwise it will look very odd at the lowest point. One shade picked out of a multicoloured design will bring harmony to the whole scheme.

Below: If your teenager craves an original headboard, encourage him or her to design their own. This headboard was made with two sheets of MDF, a design cut out and the sheets screwed together and then primed and painted in acrylic eggshell.

creating storage space

THE TINY BEDROOM

wall-to-wall

The most important item in a bedroom is, of course, the bed. It is where you spend a large proportion of your time and, if it is not comfy, poor sleep will impact on all other aspects of your life. But what if the bed is the only piece of furniture in the room? What if the room is completely filled by the bed? If your home is a studio with only a corner or platform designated for sleeping, or something out of the ordinary, such as a narrowboat or caravan, or just a very small flat, your bed and bedroom could be one and the same.

Like any piece of furniture in a

tight space, your bed needs to offer more than one function. Although you might not have any spare floor area and cannot therefore extend outwards, you will have height, and this is the dimension you should exploit.

Think of your bed as a huge storage unit with a mattress on top. Capacious drawers can be slid underneath, but be sure you have enough clearance to pull them out. There is no point in making them larger than the space you have to open them in because items will be pushed to the back, out of reach for ever. Remember, the drawers will need handles, but avoid anything that

Above: When planning under-bed storage, work out the different depths of drawers required for cushions, sheets or duvets.

Right: A simple screen that can be pulled across is a good way to section a multifunctional space. Cut-out holes prevent a claustrophobic feeling.

Far right: Luxurious wall-padding is best tackled by a professional to ensure a pristine finish.

protrudes or it could trip you up. Either cut grip-holes in the fronts or investigate recessed types of handle. These are both practical, as they will lie flush to the drawers, and stylish, with a cabin-like look.

If, for practical purposes, you can fit drawers only half the width of the bed, don't leave the other half empty. If you have a solid wooden base on your bed, you can create a hinged flap in the bed base so that you can lift the lid on the void underneath. This space can then be used to store suitcases or other bulky items. To get at this storage, you would need to pull the mattress partly off the bed to expose the flap and this could be a bit awkward, but when you live in a tiny space, give and take has to become a way of life. It is a choice between putting in some effort to have a reasonably organized and efficient home where everything has a place, or living in every night to a chaotic jumble.

PAD YOUR PAD

When the function of an item is always given priority over style, colour or texture, it is easy to end up with lots of efficient, multipurpose pieces, but few creature comforts. Function does, of course, have to come first, but this is your bedroom, the place where you expect to be able to relax and switch off. You need some softness to relieve all the usual streamlined, practical shapes and surfaces in a home, and the bedroom is the right location for a total contrast.

Generous window treatments, such as voluminous curtains, are too greedy on space, so the walls offer the only scope to create any sort of atmosphere. Dress them in something spectacular. Padded and buttoned raw silk, for example, suggests a wrap-around headboard, and creates a cushioned cocoon of luxury that is entirely different in feel to the rest of your

home. Fabric-covered walls are the ultimate indulgence, but in a tiny space it can be workable and affordable.

Make sure you can still get a sense of space beyond your door. This is vital in a confined area. Holes cut into sliding or folding wooden doors will afford a glimpse of what lies behind, while still acting as a screen, as will a semi-translucent material such as sandblasted glass or Perspex.

Sleeping above your suitcase storage, or having your wardrobe separate from the bedroom, might not be the ideal solution, but in a truly restricted space, it is a small price to pay for an indulgent bolt-hole. Whatever size your bedroom, and whatever it might lack, it need never be unsightly or uncomfortable.

SLIDING SOLUTIONS

In a very small area, convenient doors really are a waste of space. There are alternatives!

- A concertina-style door, compressed against a wall, takes up minimal space. The smaller the panels, the more compact your door will be and the less space will be required to open it.
- Sliding doors are practical for entrances or storage units, such as wardrobes. Rails fixed at right angles to the wall and covered by a sliding door will create a slimline wardrobe on a spare run of wall space.

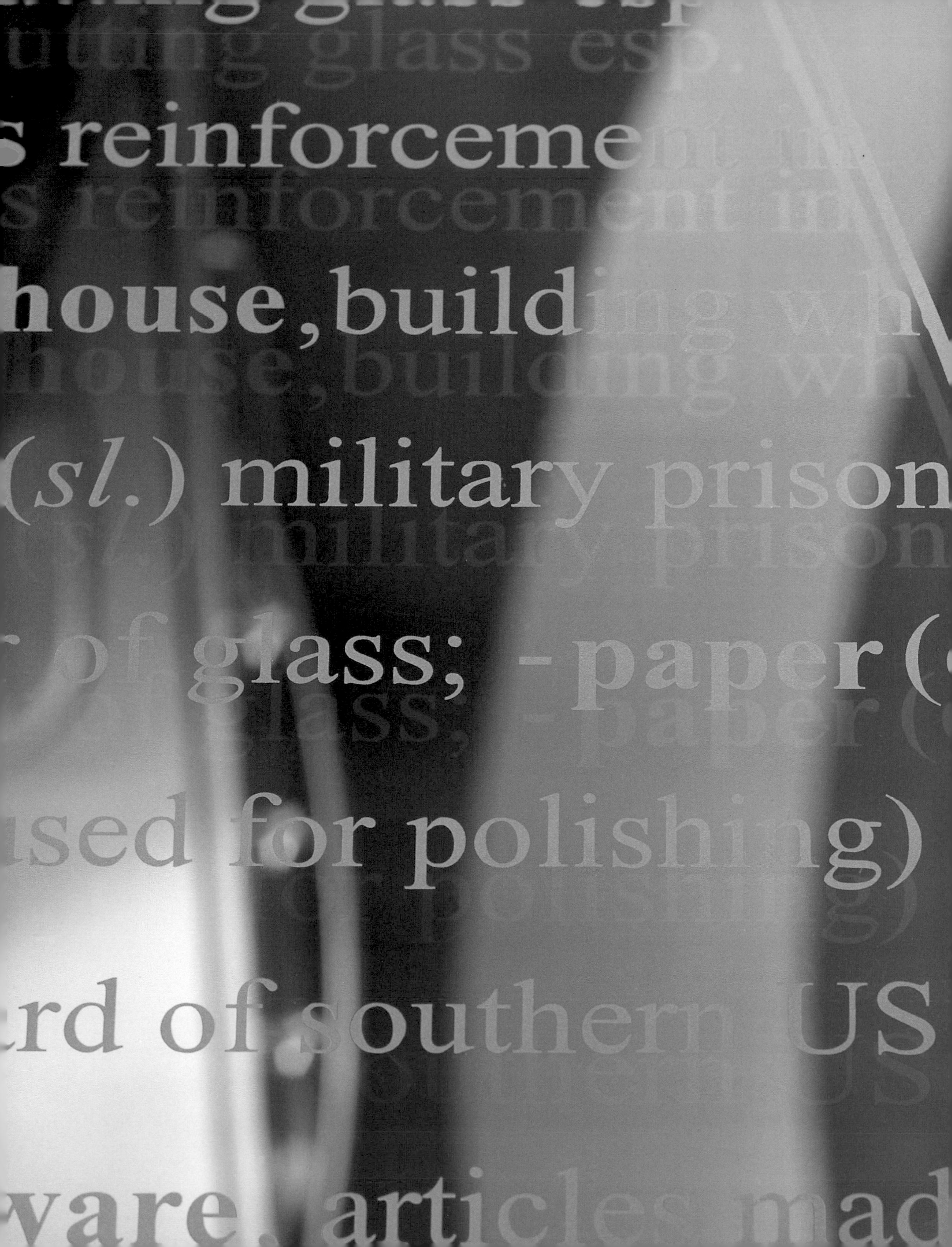

utting glass esp.
s reinforcement in
house, building wh
(sl.) military prison
of glass; -paper (
sed for polishing)
rd of southern US
ware, articles mad

connecting

spaces

Everybody's got them, but they are rarely discussed. Most of us hardly notice them, thinking they are simply the bit you pass through on the way to somewhere more interesting. But the connecting spaces in a home – the halls, landings, staircases and passageways – anticipate the places where you sleep, eat, bathe and relax. They are an integral part of the dynamics of a home and must be given the right treatment if you are to achieve continuity between rooms and a sense of wholeness.

front of house

Most homes, even the smallest, have some sort of entrance hall. Considering that this is the first place you arrive in, the impression is all too often chilly, gloomy and totally unwelcoming. Yet decorating a hall can pose some questions. As it's usually a limited space where people don't linger, it can be tempting to go a bit wild, using off-beat colours or a grand theme that you wouldn't dream of trying anywhere else. Don't let yourself be seduced down this route.

WELCOME MAT

The entrance to your home should be well lit. At a practical level, you need to be able to see properly when you come in so that you don't trip over a mat or step, and you also need to be able to identify callers at the door. Consider floor lighting as well as the more usual overhead ideas. If you have a very high ceiling, a decorative attention-grabbing light suspended in space can look stunning. It does not need to be a traditional chandelier either – there are plenty of updated variations on this theme. Alternatively, for a modern statement, suspend rows or groups of halogen spots on flexes of varying lengths (see The Light Stuff, page 46).

COME TO LIGHT

Lack of illumination is a perennial problem in hallways. A large mirror can make a tremendous difference to the illusion of light and space. If there is a window, play it up and let in as much sunshine as possible, rather than burying it behind fussy curtains or filling the ledge with ornaments.

If the view from your window is reasonable, take a fresh approach and treat it like a canvas. Paint the window-frame the same colour as the wall, so that it blends in and does not attract attention. The view will then stand out, and the light will be maximized.

Glass bricks are another useful device for a dark hall. They can be used in a window to block out an ugly vista, but not the natural light. In an upstairs property, a half-wall composed of glass bricks can make a translucent balcony, replacing a solid wall. In substituting a semi-transparent, waist-level structure for the usual floor-to-ceiling brick barrier, the whole aspect of the hall is opened up and you can now take in the height and space of the surrounding building, as well as any panoramic high-level views.

FOLLOWING THROUGH

While a hall should have its own identity, it must also have some relationship to the rooms it precedes; bear in mind that you might be able to see the hall from your kitchen and perhaps from your sitting room. Will that vista be harmonious, or will the hall seem as if it belongs in another house? Don't forget the inside of your front door either when you are planning the decor for the hall. It should blend in with the interior scheme. If your front door is varnished wood inside and out, and the hall walls and woodwork are painted, the door will look very strange from the inside.

SIMPLE SELECTION

If space is tight, a simple design will work best and a focus will be essential. At the very least you will need a console table or shelf for letters and keys. A couple of really strong, individual pieces will make a definite statement, even in a small area, whereas several little items, such as a stool, shelf, table and lamp will seem bitty and incoherent. If there is not much room to play with, keep the hall as uncomplicated and empty as possible.

OUTSIDE IN

If you have room for only two pieces of furniture, it is vital to make the right decisions. As well as looking for striking one-offs, use these objects to enhance the impression of the hall as an integral part of the larger picture. Remind yourself of the view outside, just beyond its confines, by introducing natural elements that echo shapes and colours in the garden or further afield. This could be achieved by a chair that is reminiscent of outdoor furniture, or a substantial plant or vase of flowers. The connection with the interior of your home can then be made through an item that mirrors the shape, colour or material used in another room.

The flooring can work in the same way, if you extend the choice you have made from the front door into, say, a kitchen or sitting room. Hall flooring must, of course, be practical, able to stand up to wet and mud.

FIRST FLOOR

A cream, deep-pile carpet is not a clever choice for a hall floor. As you enter your home, you will be stepping straight from the road, so pick something that can withstand dirt and damp and is easily washed. Lino-type materials or tiles are ideal.

If you really want to have carpet, a tiny mottled or flecked pattern will disguise everyday wear better than a plain one. A substantial doormat will make a

Above: A decorative piece of furniture can sometimes fit into the slimmest of spaces. In this instance, go for beauty rather than function.

tremendous difference to the amount of dirt that is trodden through the hall. Go for the fitted type if possible, rather than a loose one that lies on top of the flooring. You could also have the first metre or so behind the door laid with coir matting. This will serve as an additional dirt-retaining area before the carpet starts.

NEW FOR OLD

If you live in a period house, your hall might have a decorative terrazzo or tiled floor. These are excellent practical surfaces for this part of the house, and, if they are in poor condition, a specialist company can restore and polish them for you. They make quite a feature in a hallway, but do not feel obliged to

HALLWAY MUST-HAVES

The following touches will turn the minutest hall into a useful area.

- Electrical sockets are essential for vacuuming and for plugging in a lamp.
- A large mirror will increase the impression of light and space in a small or dingy hallway. Also, most people appreciate the opportunity to check their appearance before they rush out of the door.
- Have a table or shelf to keep a small bowl or box for keys and to prop letters for the post. But be careful. Don't leave keys anywhere within reach of a letterbox. Thieves have been known to hook them out with a stick or pole.
- A clock is always handy when you are rushing in or out. Choose something out of the ordinary to create a focal point in an uninspiring hall.
- If there is space to add a chair or bench, encourage everyone to sit down and remove their outdoor shoes in the hall. This will help to keep your carpets clean. Alternatively, keep a few pairs of loose-fitting Japanese slippers in a small box, which guests can borrow if required.

decorate the rest of the space in Victorian or Edwardian style because of an original floor. A mix of old and modern is often highly successful.

If you do not like your inherited floor, you have two courses of action. You can cover it with hardboard to protect it for a future occupant, and then lay the flooring of your choice; or you can contact a reclamation yard. If there isn't one close to you, send photos of the floor. Don't rush to accept the first offer you receive. You could achieve a substantially better price with a bit of patience. When a figure is agreed, let the experts come and lift the floor for you to minimize any damage.

WARM FEELINGS

There is nothing more depressing than coming home to a cold house. You might think that there is no point in heating a hall because you spend so little time in it. But while it does not need to be at the same temperature as, say, a sitting room, it is a false economy to let it get really icy. Cold air from the hall will just circulate through the house. A thermostatically controlled radiator will raise the temperature of the air coming in just sufficiently to combat this. Of course, the front door and any windows should be well insulated, too.

LESS MESS

Even a tiny hall can easily become a dump for shoes, bags, hats, jackets, bikes, skates and buggies. Be disciplined. If you have wardrobes elsewhere in the house, hang coats in these. After all, you can use only one coat at a time, so there is no need to have several piled up on a peg. Put up cupboard doors or a screen to mask whatever has to remain in the hall. This is the only way to avoid a really messy display which will detract from your well-planned design.

Left: The farther you can see ahead, the more spacious an area will feel. Here, glass and balcony-style partitions allow a view out to the garden.

Above: The floor at the top or bottom of a staircase is integral to its design. A detail such as this swirling shape makes a handsome finishing touch.

INDOOR GARDEN

Halls are often dominated by a staircase, and the spot underneath is a favourite location for vacuum cleaners, roller skates, power tools and an array of other household baggage. Sometimes there is just nowhere else to keep these necessities, but if you can free up this space, you can use it purely decoratively. Use the slanting line of the staircase to accommodate plants of varying heights and textures. A wide, shallow bowl on the floor can take mosses, pebbles and ground-level foliage, with taller, leafier specimens placed behind. Floor-standing plants are another reason to go for an easy-to-clean floor covering. To create an interesting mixture of colours and textures, choose your containers with care. Fibreglass 'rock lights' glowing among the plants will gently highlight the different forms.

HALL MARKS

Don't dismiss that little space behind the front door: it can be a great deal more than just the place where the stairs start to the next floor. If you embrace it and give it the recognition it merits, you will make coming home even more pleasurable. Hanging a picture, keeping shoes tucked out of sight, putting in a small radiator to generate warmth or just giving thought to how the space should be decorated will all help to create the impression you want to give of your house.

staircase study

A staircase is, of course, a functional structure that allows access from one level to another. But if it is seen solely in this light, it will be a wasted opportunity and

Above: If you can forego the storage space, you can create a fabulous focal point under the stairs. Choose unusual lighting to bring out the details.

its potential to become an area of interest, rather than just the route to somewhere else, will go unheeded. Think of the staircase as a fixed piece of furniture, and you will begin to see the possibilities.

Stairs are a unique structure in the home, the one place from which you can really appreciate and emphasize height. Painting a single wall from the ground floor up to the top in a striking colour can be all that is needed to bring this dimension into focus. A well-filled floor-to-ceiling bookcase, accessible from various levels up the stairs, will have the same effect. Spiral stairs are fascinating in their own right, and can look beautiful with stylish building materials and thoughtful lighting. The space below stairs is generally home to ironing boards, mops and other paraphernalia. Find somewhere else for these and use the vaulted area for a mini-office with a desk.

HEAVY TREADS

Stairs are subjected to a lot of wear and tear. Whatever you choose to cover them with should be

tough, non-slip and good-looking, too. Carpet or wood are the most obvious choices. If your flooring is going up more than one flight of stairs, keep to the same choice from the bottom to top for uniformity. If you change the flooring at each landing, you will break up the sense of a continuous artery twisting through the centre of the building.

Like a hallway, the staircase might seem just the place to indulge in decor you would not contemplate elsewhere. But remember that this is a connecting part of your home, which should have relevance to the rooms it adjoins. Continuity and flow will be lost if it is outrageously alien to your other choices. Keeping this in mind, two flights of steps, separated by a small landing and window, do present an opportunity for a more dramatic feature that will not impinge on other rooms. This is the perfect location for a piece of sculpture, a bust on a column, or a one-off window treatment.

A single stairway is a neat spot for a collection of photographs, hats or ceramics, which will add personality. Alternatively, highlight intrinsic details, such as an exquisitely turned Victorian balustrade, or a minimal modern chrome handrail, with well-chosen flooring and lighting. A period structure need not limit you to traditional carpet and stair-rods. Combine an original dado rail and cornicing with up-to-the-minute colours, or display old and modern art on the same wall. A mix of original and contemporary elements on the same wall is refreshing and exciting, so keep your options open.

landing stage

The landing can be one of the most peaceful havens in a busy home, so it is worth investigating if you want a quiet corner for reading or letter-writing away from the TV and the phone. A comfy armchair and small table or desk create an ideal place to relax with the newspapers or a book. Although you can arrange good lighting, it is obviously an advantage if there is already a window. If the window is little more than a slit, you might be able to enlarge it, but check out planning consent before you embark on this.

Any existing window should be the focal point of a landing and you can play up its decorative possibilities in quite simple ways. Stained glass, for example, is always appealing, and can be designed to look as traditional or as contemporary as you wish. An etched border to a pane can act like a frame around the landscape outside, making a picture without blocking natural light. This assumes that your view is worth highlighting; if it is hideous, replace the window pane with glass bricks, which will screen the vista while still letting daylight through.

tunnel vision

Connecting passageways are a common feature, particularly in older properties. Usually they are windowless and too narrow to accommodate any furniture. In this situation, good lighting is essential

both for safety and to appreciate any interest that you can introduce. If a passage ends with a door, you could put in a sandblasted glass panel to poach some daylight from the room beyond.

If passageways branch off the hall or landing, a sense of unity can be maintained by continuing the same flooring. The best way to treat a corridor is to accentuate a feeling of travelling the length of it to a destination. A series of, say, three pictures placed at regular intervals will give reference points. Pick frames of different sizes and formats, and hang them all at the same level from the ceiling. Two or three separate rugs spaced out on the floor also help visually to break up a long passage, whereas a single continuous one highlights the problem.

A single, very large vertical picture positioned halfway along the passage will accentuate height and deflect attention from the tunnel-like feel, as will painted or wallpapered vertical stripes. If you opt for this approach, choose subtle, tonal shades and a large-scale design. Narrow stripes or dazzling colours look wildly busy in a long, narrow space. A centrally positioned huge mirror will open up the most cramped corridor and give the illusion of a much wider area.

last link

When you are planning major changes in several vital rooms, it is too easy to become caught up with all that is happening and to overlook connecting spaces. But they are as much a part of the total result as a kitchen, bathroom or living room. None should become an afterthought, nor seem out of step with the general harmony and look of your home. Keep them in the forefront of your mind and you will make all the right connections.

Left: Fibre-optic lighting has been cut into each tread and the light bounced off the ends of some for a stunning effect.

the illusion of space

GLASS STAIRCASE

clear outlook

Glass is the material of the future. Research and development are now revealing its possibilities as never before. Far from being just the brittle, fragile substance we associate with tumblers or window-panes, it is now replacing wood, metal and stone in a whole range of building situations.

The beauty of glass is its most obvious quality: transparency. We now have access to a material that can bring us translucence on a truly grand scale. As the earth grows more crowded and we seek to promote the illusion of space where little exists, glass structures will become a mark of the twenty-first century. The potential is huge, so look out for glass in some surprising situations.

GO FOR GLASS

A staircase takes up a huge amount of room and is, more often than not, a large, solid construction prominently positioned in the centre of your home. There are many ways in which stairs can be integrated into the whole, but if you fancy a radical, technically progressive and architecturally enlightened approach, glass could be just what you are looking for. But if you are not prepared for serious product research, heavy financial outlay and major building upheaval,

DESIGN SOLUTIONS

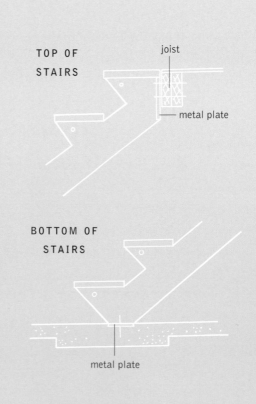

TOP OF
STAIRS

joist

metal plate

BOTTOM OF
STAIRS

metal plate

Be under no illusions! A glass staircase is not a project that should be handled by an amateur under any circumstances. It was essential to call in experts for both the technical planning and the construction work in this early-twentieth-century cottage. Their input and the materials amounted to a substantial financial outlay, but there was no other approach that could be taken. The floor had to be levelled perfectly and screed as the staircase was supported by bolts in the concrete. The treads consisted of two layers of 15mm laminated glass, each acting as a failsafe should the other break. They were mounted on a steel stringer that was bolted to a heavy metal plate at the top of the flight. Fibre-optic lighting was installed at one end of each tread, and the top surface of each tread etched to create a non-slip surface and a decorative effect.

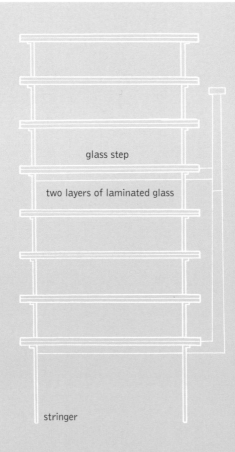

glass step

two layers of laminated glass

stringer

a glass staircase is not for you. If you are happy to put in the time, money and effort, you can achieve a unique and dazzlingly beautiful core to your home. At first glance, it might not make sense, but the smaller and more cramped your space, the more advantageous glass stairs will be. In a tiny house, for instance, one or two large focal pieces look far stronger than lots of insignificant bits that don't say anything. Although the project would eat up a disproportionate amount of your budget, it would anchor the entire scheme, and the remaining parts could – and should – be decorated as a backdrop to the centrepiece.

Visually, glass is the perfect medium for a large structure in restricted surroundings. Its transparent nature means that it appears to take up less room than it actually does, and this in turn produces the sensation of a bigger area. In a narrow location, traditional solid stairs block light and accentuate the impression of a long corridor; in the same situation, glass steps seem almost dainty and deflect attention from the limited width.

THE RIGHT TEAM

A glass staircase is no job for an amateur. The glaziers in the high street, who replace cracked window-panes, will not have the expertise, experience or tools to tackle this work, so do not even think of approaching them. Seek the guidance of a qualified structural engineer who specializes in glass construction. The contractor you choose should be completely familiar with this kind of work, and will most likely concentrate on commercial projects (see page 156). When you are budgeting for the work, be aware that if the space is particularly tight, it could take longer than you expect because there might not be room for the usual number of workers.

SPECIAL STEPS

Glass steps are fabulously decorative. Two layers of thick glass will be needed to make up each of them. This acts as a failsafe in the unlikely event of one of the layers cracking, but also adds visual interest. A fibre-optic light can be positioned in the wall at the side, just touching the edge of the stair. The result is quite magical as the tiny

Above left: A banister appears almost suspended midway between the glass steps and a transparent floor panel.

Right: The thicker your glass steps, the more handsome they will look. The safety requirement for two layers adds depth and magnifies the effect of a beam travelling from a fibre-optic light at the side.

POWDERISED

materials

lax glamorous

organic

STRUCTURAL

N
T
R

SEXY

A
U
Q

SOLID & STRONG

D
E
V
A

DELICATE & FRAGILE

transparent

R
G
N
E

formed by floating molten glass on molten ti

frozen liquid

beams travel the width of each step, and their intensity is magnified by the glass surround. Fibre-optics are a good option because they never need to be replaced, and are not disturbed by the vibration of feet going up and down the stairs. The surface of the steps can be permanently decorated with an etched design of your choice, starting right at the front edge and covering a substantial amount of the area, particularly the first few centimetres. This prevents the steps being too slippery. Your glazing expert will advise you on how much etching is needed but, if in doubt, add more rather than less.

OPEN OPTIONS

In a staircase, the clean look of glass is best offset with other modern components. Brushed steel is an ideal foil, being solid, yet with a subtle sheen. Dark-stained wood is another option. A simple shape that allows the glass steps to speak for themselves will work well. To maximize light travelling around the stairs, the framework should be as open as possible. Wherever there is a gap, you will catch a glimpse of a distant surface and reinforce the idea of something transparent yet substantial and strong. A few taut tension-wires running parallel to the handrail fill in the balustrade yet retain the impression of clear space.

CLEAR CHOICE

The tinier or narrower your home, the more glass could be the solution to some of your dilemmas. Its physical potential is huge and it can look breathtakingly beautiful and original. If you are at a loss as to how to make a lovely home out of a small, dark space, think glass and see things more clearly.

Above: The nebulous nature of glass draws attention to the solid structures that support the staircase. Each component is carefully chosen to complement the others.

Left: Bands of etching, essential for grip, span the front of each glass step. The etched lettering, although non-slip, is purely decorative.

Right: In a small home a glass staircase is an excellent option, visually absorbing minimal space. The floor panel above is etched with dictionary definitions relating to glass.

flights of fancy

DYNAMIC STAIRWAYS

long flight

If you live in an upstairs flat, a flight of steps is probably the first thing you are faced with when you open the main front door, and their potential for anything other than getting you up above might not strike you. Despite first impressions, however, stairs have plenty of possibilities.

Start by surveying from the top down and bottom up. Take advantage of the height element, which you might not have anywhere else in your home. You can, for example, make the most of the view at each end by minimizing any visual barriers. If, from the bottom step, you can see up into the rooms above, you will increase the sense of space; if, from the top step, you can catch a glimpse of garden or sky, this will have the same effect. Naturally, privacy and security are considerations, so you do need doors and walls, but they do not have to be completely solid. Consider installing clear or opaque glazed panels in doors, and walls of glass blocks, which are as strong as bricks and mortar, but translucent.

STEPS IN SPACE

A solid staircase with no gaps in it can look cumbersome, and will fill up space. If the same steps were reconstructed with open treads, the

Above left: Being in a conservatory, these ultra-modern light fittings enjoy maximum daylight for throwing out fascinating shadow play.

difference in look and feel would be amazing. Wherever light can pass unobstructed, it accentuates the size of an area, allowing you to see beyond the immediate object to a further place. An intricate structure, around which light can play, will seem less over-powering and heavy than one that blocks out light. If you have open stair treads, you will be able to look down to the floor below as you climb up and this, too, will emphasize the feeling of space all around the stairs.

By fixing a long sheet of tinted Perspex to the underside of the steps (see photograph on page 101), you can also draw attention to this view from above. Light will still come through, giving an indication of the separate space below, but you are adding an extra dimension of colour. Link the upward path to the wall at the side by painting it in the same shade.

GLOW SHOW

Badly lit stairs are a hazard, so illumination is obviously an important aspect. Ornamental lighting set into the treads themselves can have an almost magical effect as it guides your route. Fibre-optics are the ideal light-source in this situation because, once installed, they need never be disturbed as there are no expendable bulbs (see Fantastic Fibres, page 48). Positioned next to the wall at regular intervals, they will shine up in an all-day lightshow. The fan-shaped beams create a truly dramatic impact, particularly if they gleam on to a strikingly coloured surface.

HAND AND FOOT

A staircase consists of two separate elements, the treads and the balustrade. Often these match each other, for instance when both are in varnished or painted wood. However, this need not be the case. A mixture of contrasting materials can produce a set of stairs which gets noticed. For example, a glossy, dark-stained wooden tread can offset a plain, industrial-style balustrade very successfully. You can also take one element of the stairway, such as the style of a handrail, and echo it on stairs in another unconnected part of the home. This adds to a sense of unity and wholeness throughout.

THE ONLY WAY

Given the same attention as other areas of the house, stairs can form part of the total picture. If you neglect them, the time and effort lavished on other rooms will be diminished. Look upon staircases as a vital factor in your quest to personalize and unify your home.

Far left: A conservatory has to feel lush, so healthy plants are essential. Moulded bamboo chairs are a twenty-first-century update on traditional wickerwork.

Left: Fibre optics light the pathway up, even at night.

Right: The plainness of large limestone floor tiles is broken up by bands of tiny marble mosaics. Both substances are ideal low-maintenance surfaces for areas of heavy usage.

Clever positioning of a screen separates the height into two levels. From the bottom area, your attention is focused at the top of the screen rather than way above, making a more homely atmosphere in this area.

sculptural quality

SPIRAL STAIRCASES

ornamental opportunities

A conventional staircase is irrefutably a big, bulky object that can dominate an entire floor in a small home. Spiral stairs, however, could solve the problem. The very thought might call to mind a twee, wrought-iron cylinder of fussy filigree work lurking in a corner, unrelated to anything either above or below, but it does not have to be like this. If you are prepared to go in for some quite serious reconstruction, spiral steps can transform your living space.

SPACE MAKER

Changing your staircase is a practical answer to a serious space shortage. A spiral stair, with open treads and balustrade, will both physically and visually take up less room. It need not be consigned to a corner. Suspended in the centre of a room, it can take on a sculpture-like quality, marking out separate zones without being an obstructive barrier. You can see through its many gaps to the room beyond, and maybe further out to a hall or bedroom. If it leads up only one level, try to avoid lots of twists. A single swoop will look more dramatic and less tube-like, as well as being easier and safer to walk on.

Above: The spiral form is enhanced by a circular track suspended above, to which halogen spots are attached.

Right: Semi-circular layers of Perspex, glowing with the daylight behind, reinforce the sense of movement that the curves and swirls bring to this rectangular room.

LOOPING THE LOOP

Even if your room is a regular rectangle with no individuality, the spiral form will produce a wonderful sense of movement and flow, loosening the whole atmosphere. You can capitalize on this sensation by drawing attention to the coiled shape with a simple floor design at the base of the stairs. Mimic the corkscrew effect with a contrasting swirl, either painted or in tiles cut to the shape.

Clever lighting will also accentuate the architectural elegance of the structure. Halogen spots fitted to a circular track directly above the stairs will give you the delightful sensation of walking through a ring of lights as you climb up. They can also be strategically positioned to pick out details in the flooring or in the furniture below, and to create extraordinary shadow play on the walls.

Right: The steps are supported on intricately formed chrome-finish brackets, each fixed to a metal pole via a chunky metal band. A gleaming chrome-finish handrail traces the sweep of the stairs.

Below: Take advantage of the dramatic possibilities of shadows thrown by nature on the walls.

FOLLOWING ON

A spiral staircase, like any other, should relate to the surroundings it connects, but still be an object in its own right. In a newly built home, use modern materials in keeping with the setting. If you are joining, say, a sitting room with a dark-stained wood floor to a mezzanine level, opt for treads in a tough, mid-toned wood, such as untreated beech. The top surface of the step, which gets the heaviest wear, can be stained to match the floor below, leaving a border of contrasting lighter wood. You will then be able to trace the path up to meet the next level. Looking from below, you will see the paler colour of the undersides snaking up, punctuated by the balustrade fixings. A handrail, in polished chrome, for example, can prefigure detail in the room above.

STICK OR TWIST?

So if you feel that a traditional staircase is taking up more than its fair share of a limited space, something can be done. Ripping out and rebuilding is not a five-minute job, nor a cheap option, but it is well worth considering. The visual and stylistic results can be uniquely stunning. When you have only so much room, it is a pity to waste a centimetre of it.

bathroom
spaces

tale of a tub

The bathroom is something of a recent phenomenon. Within living memory, a bath was more of a chore than a pleasure, often endured crouched in a small tub of rapidly cooling water on the kitchen floor. Just a generation ago, many people were satisfied with a weekly 'bath night', which probably included a hairwash and nail-trim. The arrival of the shower in Britain made a tremendous difference to the nation's habits, and now a daily dousing in a room set aside for this very purpose is the norm.

The bathroom is an important place at both ends of the day. Many of us cannot imagine attempting anything before our morning shower ritual, complete with zesty, get-up-and-go shower gel. Besides cleansing, a shower is invigorating, wakes us up and prepares us for the day. As life has grown more pressurized, we have also rediscovered the therapeutic side of bathing, pioneered by the ancient Romans. The relaxation afforded by a soak in hot water has entered our psyche and we appreciate the benefits of unwinding in this way. The toiletries industry has expanded massively on the back of this trend, with myriad scented oils, soaps, candles, scrubs and brushes. We love treating ourselves to these items, often being seduced more by the packaging, scent and mystique of the product than what it can actually do for us.

The number, size and decor of bathrooms are now key factors in valuing residential property. As we attach more weight to their role in our lives, we hanker after a bigger space, a deeper bath, a more powerful shower and yet more litres of hot water. Appearance has become as important as the facilities. It is just possible that you are a hundred per cent happy with your bathroom, but most of us would like to make some improvements, or even start from scratch.

WATER COLOURS

Inspired by the obvious characteristics of water, blues and greens, along with fish and shell designs, are a traditional way to decorate a bathroom, and the over-all effect can either look humorous, or quite beautiful. If you decide on the shell idea, do not use real shells, starfish, coral or seahorses. These are read-ily available in shops, but are invariably sourced from already damaged reefs and plundered seabeds. If you still feel the need to purchase them, then go for the plaster versions. Alternatively, change the design.

Aside from the marine palette, bathrooms can take a range of colour choices, including some that might not immediately spring to mind.
BROWNS AND NATURALS Very restful, and a good foil for white sanitaryware.
YELLOWS Warm and inviting, and also calming.
GREENS Fresh lime or olive and khaki shades work well with white.
PURPLES AND CERISES Can look really opulent for a night-time candlelit soak. They are not quite so pleasant first thing in the morning!

Left: Fibre-optics can safely highlight detail in a bathroom, bringing out textural contrasts among the many surfaces.

Above: A monoblock tap looks far sleeker and more stylish than a pair. It is also more practical for hand washing.

If you are in any doubt about a colour, paint some on to a large piece of lining paper and stick it on the wall next to your bathroom mirror. Look at the sample over about three days and make certain you like it as much at 6.30 a.m. as you do at midnight.

Spotless bathrooms are attractive and, for this reason, white is often chosen as the dominant colour. It will always look fresh and clean, but beware of overdoing it. You could create a cold, clinical atmosphere when you are hoping to inspire a sense of purposeful energy, or tranquillity and calm. White sanitaryware and tiles work best when teamed with a contrasting shade, plus some other item of interest. Well-chosen towels, soaps and other toiletries can supply extra colour, and a substantial mirror or cabinet will provide a focal point.

DRESSING ROOM

Greenery is a superb accessory. There are plenty of plant species that thrive in a damp atmosphere, or do not need much daylight. A flourishing plant will relieve the hardness of tiles, steel and ceramics and inject life into a sometimes sterile space. If you have got room, go for an imposing, floor-standing specimen, at least 1m (3ft) high, with lush leaves. Otherwise, use the area above your head to

SIZE MATTERS

A small, poorly lit bathroom is the frustration of many homes, but there are ways to remedy this situation, if you are prepared to do without your bathroom for a few days and accept some structural alterations. Consider the following:

- BREAK THROUGH If there is a separate toilet next door to the bathroom, rip out the dividing wall. It is unlikely to be a load-bearing one, so the demolition should be relatively easy, but be sure to check with a structural engineer first. You will be amazed at the extra space you will achieve.
- BREAK UP It is perfectly possible to reorganize existing fittings to make better use of space. Simply re-positioning a bath, basin and toilet can make an enormous difference to the dynamics of a bathroom. A qualified plumber will have no trouble with this.
- BREAK OUT You cannot beat natural light, and, to get some into a small, windowless bathroom, you can replace all or part of a wall with opaque glass blocks. These offer complete privacy and the same structural support as ordinary bricks, but will allow you to poach daylight from a next-door room.
- BREAK OPEN A bathroom door that cannot be fully opened without hitting a handbasin or toilet will drive you to distraction. Change it for a sliding one, or, if possible, re-hang the existing door to open towards you, rather than into the room. Alternatively, a single door can be transformed quite easily into a matching pair of smaller ones that will take up less space. As a last resort, a rubber stopper on the floor will limit how far the door can open, so at least it does not knock against your bathroom fittings on a regular basis.

introduce hanging or trailing foliage. In both instances, make sure the container does not let you down. The key is to choose plants and pots that make a statement, and keep them healthy. A few shrivelled yellow stalks in a plastic pot will do nothing for your decor.

Pictures will also soften the edges of your bathroom. It is possible that, over time, dampness will spoil whatever is in the frames, but don't dismiss the idea altogether. Pictures in bathrooms can work surprisingly well. Simply avoid placing anything valuable in there.

Above: Accessories are a vital part of a well-designed bathroom. As well as looking good, beautiful soaps will leave a scent, while cut flowers or greenery will enliven an empty space.

BEHIND CLOSED DOORS

When you are planning storage for your bathroom, honesty is the best policy. Be realistic about how much space you are going to need. Most people have more toiletries and bath paraphernalia than they realize. Separate items that you use on a daily basis, such as toothpaste, from those, such as sun lotion or hair conditioners, that you use less frequently. You doubtless have bottles of shampoo, extra bars of soap, a new toothbrush and plenty of other bits and pieces, not to mention some first-aid equipment and possibly several aromatherapy oils and candles. Everyday toiletries need to be to hand all the time, but the rest can be stored away. A decent-sized cabinet is essential. No matter how pretty it looks, don't decide on a tiny cupboard with a single shelf. It will not hold nearly enough and will just be a waste of space. Stacks of storage boxes or baskets are also a good option, especially for awkwardly shaped articles such as spare toilet-rolls.

HOT AND COLD

The benefits of a luxurious hot soak will evaporate instantly if you step out of your bath into an icy room. Bathrooms need to be cosy. Bearing in mind that you will be undressed for most of the time that you are in the bathroom, and that it is full of cool surfaces, such as tiles and metal, the temperature should be higher than in other rooms. If you are installing a radiator, question what the heat output will be and check that it will be sufficient. Damp towels are depressing, so a heated towel-rail, which also doubles as a radiator, is an excellent addition to the bathroom.

OUTER LIMITS

The function of windows in most bathrooms is to provide light and ventilation rather than a panoramic view. Blinds make a much neater treatment than curtains, but if you use a lot of talc, beware of Venetian blinds. They will gather dust at an alarming rate. If you are not overlooked, you can probably get away with nothing at all at the windows, but panes of glass, etched, sprayed or sandblasted, will give you some privacy.

Windowless bathrooms are not uncommon, especially in flats. Good ventilation is vital to prevent damp turning into mould, so in this situation, an efficient fan is really the only answer. Sadly, a stylish wall fan

has yet to be developed, so make yours as inconspicuous as possible by removing the cover, painting the fan to blend in with the wall and replacing the cover, or partially screening it with a leafy plant.

The windowless bathroom can present another challenge in the form of an unbearably gloomy, box-like atmosphere. Good lighting can make a difference, so go for some refreshingly clear halogen bulbs (see page 48) which mimic daylight. A large mirror can also help, giving a sense of further space and reducing the feeling of confinement. Alternatively, create a focal point by directing light on to an ornament or picture. This, to some extent, can take the place of a window.

GROUND CONTROL

The choice of flooring is determined by practicalities: bear in mind that debris, such as talc, accumulates and water gets splashed around. Hygiene-wise, carpet and coir coverings are out. They will become damp and are very hard to clean thoroughly. Go for a surface that can be easily washed. Ceramic tiles are ideal, but look for a textured surface that will be non-slip. The same applies to granite or marble, which are both excellent materials in a damp environment. For more warmth under foot, cork or a lino-type material are good choices. With cool tiles, get yourself a thick, comfy bathmat to stand on. If you can afford it and are completely re-fitting your bathroom, consider underfloor heating. It is unrivalled for comfort and once you have experienced it, you will never want anything different. Also, if the bathroom is not massive, it might not work out as expensively as you think.

WIND DOWN

The bathroom has become a focus for some of our favourite day-to-day indulgences. It is a place that influences how we cope with the stresses and strains of the day, and how we drift off to sleep at night. It's a true home comfort. Let's enjoy it.

maximize space

THE TINY BATHROOM

prepare to compromise

We never seem to have enough space. It is human nature to want to spread out and occupy as much territory as possible, and possessions and lifestyle have us pushing for more. Unfortunately, the reality for many people is a constant struggle with tight corners. You might live on a houseboat, in a caravan, studio flat or tiny, ancient cottage. Whatever the situation, it's not beyond help.

FLOWING FORCES

Bathrooms are often small, and occasionally minute. It is tempting to line the walls with angular cupboards, but although storage space is necessary, this approach will shrink the room still further and contribute to a box-like feel. Flow and ease of movement are always important, but even more so in a tiny area. A continuous curving shelf at waist height will soften a stark shape and give a framework to your design. The top can be tiled with small mosaics, which won't overwhelm, and a neat, bowl-shaped handbasin without a pedestal can be integrated. The detail of the top can then be mirrored with a mini-tiled-effect flooring, which will link the two surfaces visually and instil a sense of uniformity in the room.

Above: In a small area, keep colour schemes simple and harmonious. Remember, you might well be able to see clearly from one zone to the next.

Right: A chrome hand-basin, perfectly scaled to suit this small bathroom, is integrated into the complete structure. The storage space below has no door, maintaining a smooth line and easy access.

Far right: The Japanese tub is different to a conventional bathtub in that it comes with a built-in seat and footrest. Despite being in a more upright position, a comfortable soak is possible, especially for those with a bad back.

SPECIAL SIZES

Sanitaryware generally comes in standard sizes, but your space might not permit a full-length bath. You could just accept that a relaxing soak is not for you, and limit yourself to a shower room only. On the other hand, there are fittings available, which, while they cannot actually create space, can take you part of the way. For example, a Japanese tub bath, now available in Britain, is about half the length of a normal bath but significantly deeper. An all-out stretch is obviously impossible, but you can bask up to your neck in warm water. Add a fixed tap, and a shower head on a flexible hose, which can be stored beneath the bath, and you will have as near to the best of both worlds as you are likely to achieve. The extra height of the bath means that, like the hand-basin, it can be integrated into the tiled surround, although you will need a step to help you in and out. Where every inch is vital, you will find that some styles of toilet are fractionally smaller than others from the back of the cistern to the front of the seat, so check before you go shopping, and take your tape measure with you.

SLIDING SCALE

A conventional bathroom door (see Size Matters, page 119) can present a space problem. A sliding type is a practical solution, but it need not be the plastic-covered hardboard concertina of old, which usually staggered rather than glided. Sturdy metal runners at the top and in the floor will ensure a smooth action.

For a sliding door, opt for an up-to-the-minute material. Opaque glass is an ideal bathroom surface because it is easy to keep clean and dry, and gives privacy while allowing light into the bathroom from outside, and from the bathroom into the rest of the home. Where there is no window, or a general lack of light, a glass door can make a real difference.

With a normal window, a sheet of opaque glass or Perspex will make an efficient and good-looking screen. It can be fixed to cover clear glass and is a much sleeker and less fussy choice than curtains or blinds.

HEAD ROOM

When there is nowhere to expand outwards, look up! It might not have occurred to you to locate certain fixtures anywhere other than on the ground, but when you have run out of floor space there is a whole chunk of useful emptiness at eye level and above. A radiator, for instance, can be wall-mounted (instead of floor-mounted) and double as a heat source and a towel-rail. This position might not be your first choice, but you might not have any other option.

TIGHT-SPACE TIPS

- Investigate unusual, small-size fittings and equipment. Home and design magazines are a good source for these.
- Maintain flow and unity in your design with curving contours and related patterns and materials.
- When you can't use the floor, consider using the wall space at eye level and above.
- Maximize natural or artificial light by using opaque glass or Perspex rather than solid barriers.

minimal solution

STYLISH SHOWER ROOM

shape up

Bathrooms are an important consideration when buying or selling a property, and an *en suite* main bedroom is top of many people's list. But however well-appointed a modern bathroom might be, it is unlikely to be large, and there might be room for only a shower. Don't despair: you can turn a small square box, with limited ventilation, little natural light and an absence of interesting features, into something quite spectacular. Twenty-first-century decor, along with comfort and practicality, can be injected into the most unpromising of surroundings.

Start by looking at the bare outline of your space. A dull rectangle will stay that way, no matter that tiles or towel-rail you put in it. Curves lend themselves to a bathroom, as they mark out areas within the room for, say, a shower, handbasin or toilet. Even when space is tight, you will not lose that much by creating some curved internal structures. The gap between the curved panels and the walls need not be wasted, as plumbing pipes and a toilet cistern can readily be concealed here, keeping a clean, uncluttered look in the main room. Shaped walls can indicate the different zones without the need for any sort of partition, so the open aspect is maintained.

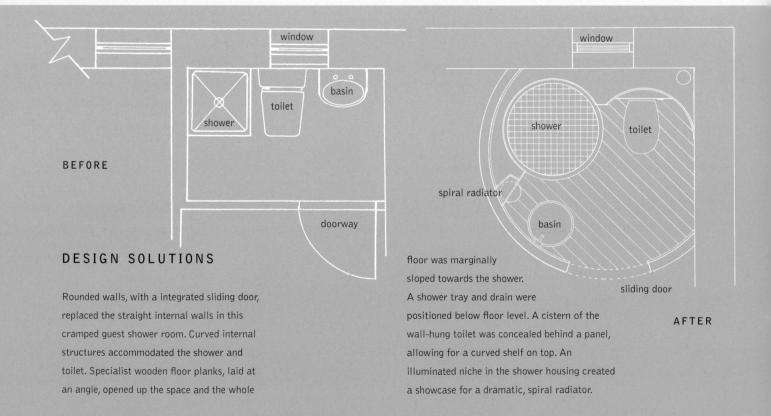

BEFORE

DESIGN SOLUTIONS

Rounded walls, with a integrated sliding door, replaced the straight internal walls in this cramped guest shower room. Curved internal structures accommodated the shower and toilet. Specialist wooden floor planks, laid at an angle, opened up the space and the whole

floor was marginally sloped towards the shower. A shower tray and drain were positioned below floor level. A cistern of the wall-hung toilet was concealed behind a panel, allowing for a curved shelf on top. An illuminated niche in the shower housing created a showcase for a dramatic, spiral radiator.

AFTER

Stepping over the side and into a shower-tray before pulling a curtain or door closed behind you is the norm when you shower in Britain. But if the entire floor is marginally sloped towards the drain below the shower head, the area around the shower can be left flush with the rest of the floor. This means that the little wall that usually projects several centimetres up from the ground around the shower tray can be dispensed with. If the surrounding materials can cope with a drenching, then an enclosed shower, plus the curtains or a screen, becomes unnecessary.

Where there is obviously going to be a lot of splashing about, tiled walls are the best bet. Gone are the days of patterned or plain ceramics and not much else. There is now a world of choice in shapes, sizes and finishes for tiles, with materials such as limestone, slate and glass becoming more

accessible. These developments have opened up further design possibilities as we are no longer bound by manufacturers' colour selection. Translucent glass tiles come in a variety of textures and shimmering iridescent finishes that are reminiscent of mother-of-pearl. As they have no intrinsic colour of their own, background colour that shows through can be produced by using a pigmented adhesive. Stick to one shade, or try different tones for a subtle variation around the room. Grouting, too, is no longer limited to white or grey. Choose a colour that complements your design.

GLASS ACT

Glass is also at the forefront of today's bathroom fittings. Its tough surface and clear or semi-opaque nature make

it both practical and contemporary. Improvements in the manufacturing of glass products means that items such as handbasins, which were beyond most pockets a decade ago, are now far more affordable and look extremely chic. There is a massive range of glass accessories now on sale in high streets, including toothbrush holders, soap-dishes and shelves. Choose smooth, softly rounded shapes, avoiding sharp angles and unforgiving corners. The reasonable prices of smaller articles mean that you could probably update these components more frequently to keep a fresh edge to the overall look.

OFF THE FLOOR

The aim is to keep the room as clear as possible. With this in view,

Above left: The appearance of textured glass tiles is altered by mixing different pigments into the adhesive behind them. A highly individual look can be created using a variety of shades around the room.

Right: Within a square room, curved structures create mini-enclosures for the shower and toilet. Tiling only certain areas makes these beautiful glass tiles more affordable.

concealed plumbing and discreetly styled wall-hung sanitaryware will give you the best look. If you can see underneath objects to the space below, you will not get the impression of a small area cluttered with furniture. This is also practical, being easy to clean.

Be realistic when thinking about storage in a small bathroom. Look out for storage baskets or canvas containers that you can move about, hang up or stack as you wish. Spend some time on the details, such as the type of basket, tone and texture of towels and arrangement of stylish soaps and bottles, and the entire design will come to life.

ALL MOD CONS

Think about the neatness of other fittings, too. A monoblock tap, which has a single spout mixing hot and cold flows together, will always look more streamlined than two separate taps.

It will also ensure that your hands do not suffer regular freezing or scalding washes. Radiators no longer need to be ugly white blocks that fill up walls. Investigate slim upright shapes and a variety of colours and finishes. Today, the humble radiator can be a showpiece of up-to-the-minute design form, so if you go for a really beautiful one, draw attention to it with lighting, which also throws interesting shadows on to the wall. Even your toilet can have panache. Brushed metal or shiny chrome, topped with a Perspex toilet seat, make a hi-tech alternative to the traditional, often fussy porcelain with a predictable wooden or plastic seat.

WATERWAYS

Once you have experienced a really powerful shower, you will never be happy with anything less. If you have trouble getting yourself moving first

thing, it is one of the best investments you can make. If you have a small bathroom and nowhere to enjoy a proper soak, it is well worth going for the biggest shower-head you can afford, and a first-class electric pump. Be prepared to spend up to £500 on a pump. It is the only way to get a really forceful flow. (A plumber might tell you that your home is not suitable for a large pump, but unless you live in a flat with a communal water system, this is unlikely to be true. The chances are you just need to find a more experienced plumber.)

The location of the pump is important. Have it fitted as near as possible to the shower, but not in a bedroom or on the floor (which it will vibrate through). The pump can be very noisy when in action, so if possible position it inside a cupboard and soundproof it if necessary.

Left: Flowers and greenery are often limited to a solitary pot-plant, or left out of the bathroom altogether. Cut stems introduce a special freshness and life.

Below: Give radiators sculpture-like status and highlight the decorative effect with lighting.

STEPPING OUT

Shower-room flooring should be comfortable under foot, easy to clean and able to withstand water. There are various options to consider, such as tiles, rubber or vinyl-type materials and underfloor heating (see Ground Control, page 121).

A wooden floor is appealing, but you might be put off by the thought of applying regular coats of varnish, or resigning yourself to inevitable water-marks after a few months. The solution can be found on the decks of yachts throughout the world and it's called iroko. Iroko is a hard wood, ideally suited for use in wet surroundings. It needs no seal or varnish and will not mark. It just turns darker when in contact with damp, while remaining non-slip.

It is not a cheap option, and if you set out to source it, be on your guard. Make absolutely sure before you commit that you are buying from a reputable merchant and that the wood has come from a sustainable plantation, not a wild rainforest. If you are not a hundred per cent confident of your source, choose an alternative flooring. Don't perpetuate trade that damages the environment.

LAST DROP

Bathrooms and shower rooms are not the functional, inhospitable little cubicles they used to be. They are where you go to be refreshed and revitalized to face the demands of the day. They are a place to unwind and pamper yourself in comfortable and inspiring surroundings. They can play a vital part in the way you feel at either end of the day. They are often a bit small, but they need never be insignificant.

Above: This chrome toilet is similar to those found on aeroplanes, but is topped with a Perspex seat.

Below: This circular grid lies above a drainage tray. Its look is inspired by wooden grids used on yachts. Iroko wood is ideal for withstanding water.

Below: A huge showerhead installed directly overhead on the ceiling has the effect of a powerful cascade from a waterfall.

no boundaries

EXTRAORDINARY *EN SUITE*

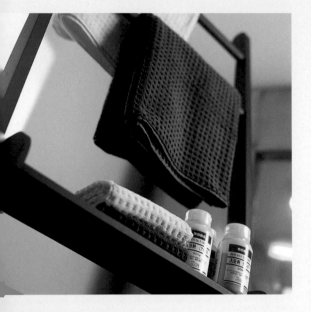

soap and water

If you are looking to increase the value of your property, an *en suite* bathroom is one of the best improvements you can make. Indeed, it is now extremely rare to find a newly built home without one.

HIS 'N' HERS

Both men and women have careers outside the home, and it is usual these days for couples to unwind together after a long day. What could be more inviting than to relax on a comfortable bed after a soak in a warm bath with delicious scented oils? In the modern *en suite* set-up, the bathroom and bedroom are amalgamating into one space, with the two functions delineated only by a change of flooring. The concept of a double bedroom and a tiny, separate bathroom with walls and doors in between is fading in favour of a far more open layout, with each area commanding a similar proportion of the space.

By allowing more space, you can spoil yourself with a generous bath for two. The ultimate indulgence is a circular tub, not much smaller than your bed, from where you can see the entire room. Set fibre-optics into the floor around it for a safe and truly modern alternative to the candlelit bath (see Fantastic Fibres, page 48).

A really powerful shower positioned

DESIGN SOLUTIONS

Although it was not large, this *en suite* bathroom (part of the bedroom on page 84) felt generously proportioned. Tiny, circular mosaic tiles covered the floor and walls seamlessly – and the only barrier was a wall of opaque glass blocks – so the effect was as open as possible. Opaque Perspex disguised the uninteresting windows, while still letting in both air and light. The twin spheres of the copper washroom pod and sumptuous bath added to a sense of movement and were mirrored in the curved wall and rounded edge where the tiles and bamboo flooring met. Fibre-optic lighting studded the floor around the bath and a powerful shower and statuesque towel rail reinforced the over-riding sense of luxury. Inside the copper pod, a false wall hid the toilet cistern and created an extra storage shelf.

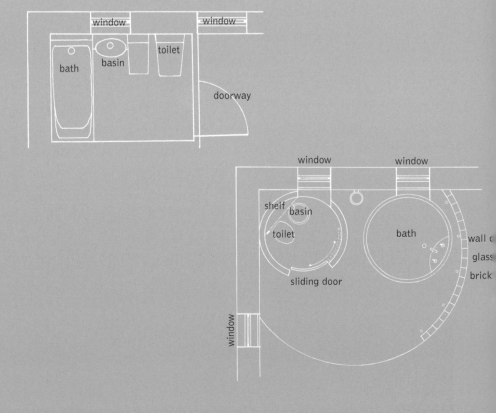

above the bath will give you the nearest you will get to a drenching under a waterfall (see Waterways, page 126). As long as surrounding surfaces are waterproof and the floor is slightly sloped towards a drain, you can stand under a steaming or freezing torrent and splash to your heart's content. Compare the freedom and exhilaration of this to hunching under a half-hearted trickle enclosed by Perspex or a damp and clammy nylon curtain.

If you have the space, emphasize it with a free-standing, full-height towel-rail. A ladder-like style will draw the eye upwards. What you put on it is important, so treat it as a display item. Beautiful bathroom accessories are all you have to dress and personalize this space, so spend time picking out less obvious colours and textures for towels and bathmats. Go for good-looking soaps and brushes, which balance some of the more functional, everyday toiletries that have to have their place.

WALL OF LIGHT

No matter how close you and your partner are, there is always a need for some seclusion. Walls are the enemy of light and spaciousness, and when these elements are in short supply, you need other options to act as a screen. If your *en suite* bathroom is in danger of being dark, consider a wall of glass bricks. A pale green tone, sandblasted, is a good choice. A glass wall is completely opaque, maintaining privacy, yet allowing daylight to glow through to remind you of the space beyond. Take the idea a step further and put a slight bow into the shape of the wall. This will create an extra effect of a white glow where light hits the centre of the panel, flanked either side by the concentrated green glass, unsuffused by illumination from outside.

COOL COPPER

Doubtless, in an open room you will wish to screen off the toilet. A flexible structure, such as a cylindrical cubicle with a sliding door that does not protrude unnecessarily, is ideal. As this whole section of the home is about pleasure and leisure, make it look really special. A basic plywood frame can be wrapped in the thinnest of copper sheeting to make a glowing, burnished pod that becomes a private washroom when required. An incandescent blue cathode tube placed against the metallic surface inside will produce an almost alien glimmer from within.

Building this is quite an ambitious task, but it can be achieved with a little inside knowledge. Be prepared to take some time to track down the right source for the metal sheets, and also to identify the most suitable grade. Phone the metal supply companies listed in

Above left: Where space allows, a free-standing towel-rail can almost act as a display unit for attractive toiletries.

Right: Copper naturally assumes a greenish patina over time, so works comfortably with green glass bricks. Fibre-optics set in the floor send beams up through the curved wall.

Below: Wet and dry areas within one room are separated by a change in flooring. Each material has been thoughtfully selected for its beauty and practicality.

Yellow Pages, and explain exactly what you want to do. Listen to advice and ask to see sample pieces of the various thicknesses available before you buy anything. The heavier your choice, the more expensive it will work out, but you will probably be best off with the finest, most pliable grade. Measure the area you want to cover so that you know roughly how much copper you will need.

Next, you need to find a company experienced in working with copper sheets (check in *Yellow Pages*). These firms, called metal fabricators, normally fit out bars and other public places, so keep your eyes open and do a little detective work. You will be amazed what you can discover. Expect your fitter to spend one or two days wrapping the pod, depending on its size, and make sure you know exactly what the cost will be before you get started.

Copper is notorious for reacting badly in damp conditions, but there is a foolproof method of preserving its warm, gleaming surface in a bathroom. It can be sealed with acrylic varnish, but this is not a job to tackle on a spare evening. The varnish has to be sprayed on to avoid leaving brushmarks. First, you will have to clean the copper until it is as perfect as you can make it. Any remaining marks will be sealed in under the varnish for good. Either hire spraying apparatus, or use a canister. Whichever route you choose, be very careful and very sensible. Excellent ventilation and a face-mask are vital. If the room has small or no windows, seriously consider hiring an oxygen tank along with the rest of the equipment.

Clear the area and cover every surface, including walls and floor, with plastic sheeting. Any exposed parts will receive a light film of varnish which you won't be able to remove. The

Above: The wall of glass bricks serves to divide the bathing area from the rest of the bedroom and brightens up an otherwise dark corner by allowing light to come through.

Left: Copper heaven...but hold your nerve. An ambitious design will fail unless it is executed wholeheartedly. The structure looks so stunning because the copper covers every possible part.

Right: An uninspiring window has been covered with white Perspex, taking on the appearance of a light while still functioning as a ventilation source. A further glow comes from a blue cathode tube light, gleaming against the copper wall.

whole process might take a couple of days, during which the bathroom will be out of action. Be under no illusions: this is not an undertaking for the faint-hearted, but if you do go for it, the results are more than worth the grief. Copper is a beautiful, shimmering surface that embodies warmth and originality.

DISCREET CHARM

A striking focus, such as an enormous, attention-seeking bathtub, or a glimmering copper cubicle, deserves centre stage in your *en suite* bathroom, so create maximum impact with careful choices around large pieces. Flooring, as it is such a large surface, can often define the whole ambience of a room, but here you want a backdrop rather than a feature. Tiles are the perfect solution to splashes of water both under foot and on walls. A simple white ceramic mosaic of

small, round tiles, grouted in contrasting charcoal grey, will set off large items in the room without drawing attention away from them. When you study it, you will appreciate detail that is barely noticeable from a distance. Inconspicuous decoration like this, which yields only to close inspection, brings an extra layer of richness and complexity to your design.

Likewise, a radiator can be chosen either for its style or self-effacement. A tall, narrow, spiral shape will complement other rounded forms but, chosen in a dark grey finish, it can tuck into a corner almost unseen at first glance. Wall-hung sanitaryware in simple shapes minimizes clutter and frees up floor space, so you can clean thoroughly around and underneath it. You will also gain more impression of the full extent of the room. A wall-hung toilet with a concealed cistern will usually have slimmer-shaped

workings than a floor-mounted one. This can be boxed in for a clean streamlined feel, and an extra shelf can be created on top. Natural touches, such as a smooth wooden handbasin, loofahs and beautiful hand-crafted soaps, add mellowness, as do soft, textured towels in complementary shades that are easy on the eye. Opt for a monoblock tap for neatness.

WATER-WORLDS APART

Take on board the concept of the *en suite* as an integral part of the ritual of relaxation, from undressing to bathing and then to bed. Lift this element of your routine right out of the ordinary and take it a world away from the far-too-common, exasperatingly minuscule construction behind a partition wall in the corner of the bedroom. Where would you rather unwind?

Right: This beautiful wooden handbasin, made from layers of beech ply, feels incredibly smooth to touch and makes a striking contrast to shiny copper, chrome and white mosaics.

Above: Using the same mosaic tiles on walls and floor gives a oneness to the design. A semi-circular box conceals pipework and the toilet cistern, while the top has been wrapped in copper to form a shelf.

Right: Circular mosaics, like the more usual square ones, are applied in made-up sheets, approximately 90sq cm (14sq in). Being ceramic, they can cover both floor and walls and their discreet pattern forms the perfect backdrop for gorgeous fittings.

future spaces

How do trends evolve? Where do fashions come from? Who dictates that this colour is 'in' and that colour 'out'?

Trends emerge as a reaction to events or feelings that affect us. No one can stop them coming and going, and the strongest ones somehow infiltrate worldwide, so that the same moods translate themselves into clothing, style or tastes in the Western sphere of influence at roughly the same time. A country or culture might become the focus of attention for political or artistic reasons, but its music, food, dress and flavour might then permeate other cultures and a trend for the Oriental look, or the Australian-surfer-style, is born. Global events can change people's attitudes to problems such as the destruction of our environment, and a whole way of life comes about, from wearing fashionable earthy shades and rejecting fur to recycling in a committed manner.

It's true that there is very little that is new in the world. Trends merely focus attention on a style that already exists, but isn't currently in the public consciousness. The constant revamping of fashions of the Twenties, Forties, Sixties or Seventies shows this. Each time an era is revived, the looks are modified to appeal to today's consumers, while the essence remains.

The three trends that follow here, the New Millennium Kitchen and the Organic and Glacial directions, are the conclusions from several months of research. Computer and kitchen appliance manufacturers, food technologists, telecommunications specialists and a host of other experts have all been consulted for their views on how products and lifestyles will develop over the next twenty years.

Changes such as global warming and overcrowding, which we already see happening to our Earth, emerge as key to these predictions, as we adapt to cope with new situations. Awareness of the environment is already manifesting itself on the catwalk and in the stores in the explosion of floral designs and patterns inspired by natural objects such as fossils and feathers. Transparency, the heart of the Glacial trend, is already a strong look in home accessories and is set to grow even more important.

Not everything you find in the following pages will definitely happen. Some ideas might never appear in your home, or might develop in a different way. None of us can see the future with total certainty. We can be sure only of where we are today, and where we would like to find ourselves tomorrow.

Both this delicately formed Perspex chair and London's Millennium Dome behind it are symbolic of the future of design. Which will survive as a classic and which will disappear for ever?

new millennium kitchen

THE WAY AHEAD

Above: Near-future designs hold a combination of man-made, translucent and natural materials.

one step beyond

People used to imagine that by the close of the twentieth century, we would all be wearing silver space-suits, buzzing around in flying saucers and living on a single nutritionally balanced tablet instead of three meals a day. Human life has been evolving since the dawn of time, but today our world is changing more rapidly than at any other time in our history. Technology is advancing at such an awesome rate that new products become obsolete within months, superseded by something even more powerful, clever or quick. Sometimes we struggle to keep up with the monsters we have created. With e-mail, for instance, communication that might have taken days by post now takes seconds and we must be ready to respond immediately.

In our daily lives we are both helped and harassed by the twenty-first century, exhilarated and exhausted in equal measure. As we adapt our homes to the future, we will focus on two forces – one drawing us into the comfort we knew before the explosion of technology, the other pulling us forward to embrace the challenges of the new millennium.

It is, of course, impossible to predict the future with any certainty, but we can envisage what will become

DESIGN SOLUTIONS

This kitchen design was a vision of a typical kitchen twenty years from now. Many of its basic components are familiar, but have been altered subtly to meet the predicted changes in our lifestyle and environment. The hob is flanked by worktops, but they are mobile glass units giving greater flexibility than current static furniture. The hob itself is also mobile and can be pushed up and out of the way if required. Today's fixed wall cupboards have been superseded by a far more capacious sliding storage unit, as many items will be bought be in bulk. The seating area for family meals is reduced as individuals keep to their own schedules, and seats have to double as storage boxes. A fridge, dishwasher and drawers are integrated into an undulating wall and a focal point is the huge interactive TV screen.

achievable. We can also forecast some of the global changes that will occur and how our homes might adapt to them. Twenty years hence, the world will be a different place. Facilities such as the Internet, which were once the stuff of sci-fi novels, have now become commonplace realities. Witness the advent of the mobile phone which, in the space of a decade, has evolved from a James Bond-like fantasy gadget to a lifeline and mainstay of business and social communications.

MICRO CHIPS WITH EVERYTHING

Computers will play a pivotal role in the home of the future. You will probably have at least one screen in each room, and they will be linked so that instead of shouting from the bed-room down to the kitchen, you will simply flick on your screen to talk to your partner or the kids. The screen

will be prominent, possibly like a huge picture on the wall from where you can see and be seen in any part of the room. It will also connect you to a host of useful interactive locations. Imagine your favourite TV chef talking you through a recipe, pausing whenever you get left behind, showing you the complicated bits a second time and then waiting till you are ready before moving on to the next stage. It could happen…

Many day-to-day operations in the kitchen will also be controlled by computers. As well as obvious tasks, such as the timing of lighting or heating, a computer will know when the dishwasher is full and switch it on. It could read what is in the fridge, suggest menus you can make and produce a shopping list when stocks run low. Beyond this, it could be linked up to your chosen supermarket so that your requirements can be

ordered and delivered straight to your door, as needed. It will replace a notepad or blackboard, so instead of jotting down a reminder to buy more cat food, you will just tell your computer and it will remember.

A computer might be able to see not only into your fridge, but also into you. This might sound spooky, but it is actually a real and useful possibility. A sensitive pad, set into a worktop or wall, would be able to ascertain your health and nutritional needs from your skin. The trace of moisture from a hand placed on its surface would trigger a read-out of the foods required to re-balance your intake. If, for example, you had been living on hamburgers over the weekend, it might suggest a concentrated fruit breakfast on Monday morning, while if you had been seriously dieting, it might suggest a higher level of carbohydrates and calories.

Right: Highly efficient storage can be achieved with closely situated shelves that move to allow access by means of a winding mechanism. The large, slim TV monitor hangs like a picture on the wall, and below it a glass panel gives a view of greenery beyond.

Below: The bamboo flooring has etched glass inserts, revealing the glow of luminous gravel below.

white out

The size and appearance of appliances will evolve, too. Current trends are already heralding the demise of traditional 'white goods', some of which have hardly altered since the 1950s. Those white metal cubes with sharp corners are becoming rounded, more friendly shapes, and taking on some adventurous colours. We are familiar with small items, such as kettles, in brightly coloured finishes, but these are now being developed in transparent materials, so you can watch the water boiling and the bread browning. Manufacturers predict that the arrival of see-through fridges or washing-machines is not far away, and that as the idea of non-white appliances becomes more accepted, you will have a facility to change their colour electronically at the touch of a button. Clip-on casings in hundreds of designs and shades will also be on the market, so you could just buy a new cover whenever you fancied a change.

future feeding

Food, of course, will continue to be the focus of the kitchen, but changes that are already happening in our eating habits will have an impact on our daily routine. In Britain £1 million per day is spent on chilled prepared meals, a concept unheard of fifteen years ago. Likewise, we also buy litres of bottled water every week. The average family fridge will clearly have to grow in capacity to accommodate this demand. Organic produce is also sure to increase in popularity as we learn more about what we eat. And because this food is as nature intended, it does not keep for as long as some genetically modified goods, and we will need yet more refrigerated space to prolong its freshness. Alternatively, we could see the arrival of 'super' vegetables, genetically altered to have an almost infinite shelf-life, which we might buy in bulk to put in the fridge. We can only guess how they might taste.

Further pressure on space will arise from the need to recycle household waste in an organized and committed

Above: Drawers are entirely integrated into the wall. The raw, rustic bark-styling is a strong reminder of the natural world.

Right: The fridge of the future might take on the role of a larder, storing ingredients such as herbs and cooking oils. An attachment might possibly convert a cupboard into a cold-store.

Above right: This mobile unit incorporates storage space in its curvaceous design. Pads that sense our nutritional needs would also be built in.

Far right: The cooker is pulled down when needed and lined up with the food preparation area.

way. At the very least, it could become a legal obligation to recycle glass, cans and paper, with fines for non-compliance. Compost heaps and wormeries might become common features outdoors.

TROLLEY DASH

In the future it is unlikely that we will go shopping as frequently as we do now. In the past, as the use of preservatives and refrigeration increased, the daily trip to buy fresh meat and bread became a weekly chore; now we purchase certain toiletries and household goods on only a monthly or quarterly basis. Time is precious, so buying in bulk is a natural progression. This obviously necessitates more storage space. The traditional wall and base kitchen units could be replaced by larger, highly efficient, floor-to-ceiling cupboards seen only in commercial situations at present.

COOKING 'EGGS'

The humble cooker has hardly altered for more than a generation, but change is afoot.

- In line with the trend towards more flexibility in the use of available space, the cooker of the future could be a large, egg-shaped piece suspended from the ceiling.
- The main part of the 'egg' would house an oven and hob, while the top portion would contain an extractor hood.
- Hydraulic pulleys would draw the oven down for use and it could be pushed back out of the way after.
- Naturally it would probably be any colour but white.

space age

Space is one commodity we can't control and there is simply never enough. In the kitchen of the future, we will have to use space even more efficiently than we do today. As base cupboards with fixed worktops become a thing of the past, streamlined mobile units that incorporate sinks and food preparation areas will take their place. A pair of worktops might have a central fixed point around which they could rotate independently. They could therefore be set at right-angles to one another, in a straight line or any configuration in between. Plumbing could be installed in the central structure, and water piped around the circumference of the worktops to the sinks and taps at the furthest points. This would be done through flexible hoses, similar to those currently used in hairdressing salons, rather than rigid water-pipes. This kind of plumbing would not meet current health and safety requirements as the pipework for domestic waste must be sealed to a very high standard. However, as mobility becomes more important, supple materials and technology will no doubt develop to meet the demand.

Precious space in locations we just do not think about at the moment will be pressed into service to meet our ever-growing needs. The kitchen floor might be built up artificially to create a useful void underneath. Seating, in the shape of simple chunky stools, will then be stored below floor level, and could be simply raised by a system of hydraulics when required. When not in use, the tops of the stools would fit seamlessly into the floor. Multipurpose rubber flooring would be suitable as both seat covers and for use under foot. If the stools themselves were hollow, they could form useful under-floor storage crates. There would also be less need for fixed seating as the sit-down family meal becomes even more of a rarity and individuals tend to snack alone to suit their separate timetables.

BACK TO NATURE

Amid our twenty-first-century high-tech whirl, there is going to be a yearning to hold on to our roots. No matter how advanced we become, primal instincts remain with us and we cling to reminders of the real, natural world beyond the computerized and manufactured environment we have grown to accept.

This could manifest itself in the types of materials incorporated into the kitchen. Wood, especially in a raw state, will be popular. Some furniture could almost look as if it is built from

Above: Stools double as below-floor storage crates that are raised by hydraulics when needed for seating. Their rubber seat covers become part of the flooring when they are lowered.

IN THE COOLER

Global warming seems virtually unstoppable, for now at least, and in twenty years you could expect to feel some of its effect in the kitchen.

- A rise in temperature means that all perishable food will have a shorter life, needing to be stored in a colder fridge than we are used to at present. Even foodstuffs we currently think of as non-perishable, such as tea, sugar and flour, will be affected, and the old-fashioned idea of a larder could be resurrected as a cool storage area for dry goods that will no longer last in an ordinary cupboard for any length of time.
- Global warming could also cause a whole new range of insects not usually associated with Europe to arrive. Mesh-fronted bug-resistant units might become the norm.

logs, and bark will be used as a textural contrast to streamlined steel or glass surfaces. Bamboo will become totally accepted as an environmentally friendly and highly practical alternative to wooden flooring. A kitchen sink, like a bowl or bucket, might be made from wood rather than metal. Style and interest will spring from the contrast of traditional and modern materials. Organic, curvaceous shapes will be juxtaposed with chunky, industrial-style details.

Limestone and other natural substances will appear in worktops and under foot. Glass, too, should come into its own as a superbly tough, hygienic and handsome kitchen surface. As well as appearing on worktops, it could feature in floors, in the form of translucent illuminated panels, perhaps set over a scattering of luminous gravel chips, with a decoratively etched, non-slip surface.

future in focus

Much of this picture might never materialize, but if you follow a trend to its natural conclusion, you can gain a fair idea of what the future might hold for our homes. Some of the suggestions might seem far-fetched, or even inconceivable, but remember, many items now in everyday use hardly existed ten or twenty years ago. It sounded incredible that a two-minute blast of electromagnetic radiation could transform chilled food into a piping-hot meal. We call it a microwave. Our world is a rapidly changing place and, in the absence of a reliable crystal ball, you need somehow to be prepared.

Left: Economy of space in the kitchen of the future will demand mobility from most items. A cooker could perhaps be raised up or even pushed into the ceiling when not in use.

Right: Substantial legs and castors support the weight of the mobile work area.

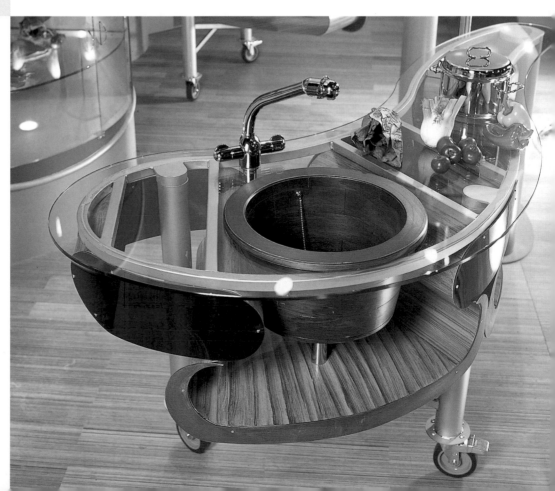

organic living

man-made marvels

Manufactured goods were the technological wizardry of the 1950s and 60s. Man-made materials were considered far more desirable than the traditional ones, which had been around for centuries. In the home, wood, stone, leather, glass and natural fabrics all gave way to more expensive man-made equivalents, which were thought to be superior in quality, easier to maintain and thoroughly 'modern'.

This trend has come full circle, with a backlash against imitation, and a desire for the genuine article. We now crave French oak flooring or silk curtains where wipe-down plastic and easy-care polyester were once the peak of desirability.

THE REAL THING

Today, surrounded as we are by the instantaneous effects of microchips, we value a sense of history. While the vogue for faithfully restoring a Victorian or Arts and Crafts interior is waning, the appeal of original materials is becoming increasingly strong. We cheerfully pay more for second-hand flooring from an old school gym than for new wood because we relish its unique, lived-in

Above: This flooring material is a new product, not yet on sale in the UK, and is made entirely from crushed recycled drinks cartons.

Right: Bamboo cladding, which takes the place of a picture, introduces texture to a wall.

Far right: Large designs painted or stencilled on to a blank wall work successfully when the colours are in harmony with the rest of the room.

Below: Man-made concrete balls mixed with real cobblestones – which are old and which new?

character. Glass mosaic tiles, with their echoes of ancient Rome, bring quality into a bathroom in a way that modern ceramics cannot. A pure linen tablecloth, no matter how well used, will always have a style and presence that is far richer than any synthetic fabric.

The desire for something real and elemental rather than manufactured is reflected on the catwalk, too. Witness the emergence of outdoor and sports-related clothing, or the growing prominence of all shades of green, from dazzling lime to sludgy khaki. These trends infiltrate our homes as well as our wardrobes, and although we might not be fully aware of the cross-over, they become part of how we live, not just how we dress.

TAKE IT HOME

Regardless of its size or style, you can bring the ideas of permanence, purity and the natural world into your own living room. Many items available on the high street have been inspired by this mood, but they are by no means necessarily 'natural' or rustic-looking. Raw or recycled materials can be adapted in ingenious ways. Did you know, for instance, that you can readily buy a durable and attractive woven floor rug made from paper? Or that foil-lined drinks cartons can metamorphose into sheets of hard-wearing flooring?

A walk by the sea, through a forest or fields, or over rocks can inspire you to bring reminders from the outdoors into your home. You can give green plants the status of furniture by going for a few statuesque, floor-standing specimens with large sculptural leaves to give a the room jungle flavour. Terracotta-coloured plastic containers will jar, so swathe your plant pot in an untreated fabric such as hessian, or

GREEN ISSUES

A palette drawn from rock, wood and greenery might sound less than inspiring, but you can produce something modern, subtle and surprisingly varied from this.

- Explore the whole green spectrum, as well as browns, greys and all shades in between, and don't be afraid to add a splash of something unexpected.
- Geometric black and white suggests the technological age and, used in a small section as a total contrast to the main inspiration, will highlight and strengthen the overall message.
- Create pattern with rounded, cell-like shapes that hark back to the simplest life-forms, and also forward to the microchip.

ELEMENTAL ESSENTIALS

- Rounded shapes for furniture and walls.
- Natural, recycled or sustainable materials, for example, bamboo, stone, glass, paper.
- Colour inspired by the natural outdoor world.
- Greenery and water.

choose ceramics with their associations of clay and firing. Include a miniature water feature, animated with air bubbles, for true dynamism. You can also surround yourself with the atmosphere of a woodland, using bundles of twigs from a florist. Two rows of tension-wires suspended across the ceiling will allow you to interweave the twigs from each side so that they lock together in the middle, forming a tree-tunnel reminiscent of the cocoon-like depths of the forest, a world away from city life.

SHAPES OF THE FUTURE

Organic forms tend to be fluid and curvy. You will see very few straight edges or sharp corners, so keep this in mind when it comes to furniture. Choose rounded chairs in natural materials, such as rattan, that look almost as if they grew up from the floor, and let them wrap around you, so you feel cosy and secure. Although you might consider concrete the epitome of a modern building material, it can be moulded into any shape you wish, while keeping a rough, unfinished surface and a stone-like quality. It can be used to introduce waves and twists that mimic ancient fossils.

You can even add some shape to flat surfaces. For example, the zigzag of a screen can be used purely for decorative purposes, not just when you have something to hide. The simple introduction of a vertical plane will break up a dull space and is especially effective for adding interest to a bland corner. Alternatively, consider using some bamboo cladding to create a textured wall. Grouping similar items together is also an effective way to introduce a variety of height and texture. A cluster of pots or cobbles of different sizes will breathe life into a lacklustre space as well as add interest.

welcome to the oasis

There can be a sanctuary within your home, where the desire for natural simplicity is fulfilled, a place where you want to do little more than curl up into an all-enveloping chair and switch off your mind along with your mobile phone. The living room can offer you refuge from modern stresses and allow you space to recharge your batteries. Surround yourself with natural forms and colours and materials that are easy on the eye and take a rest from the present day. You will emerge refreshed and ready for whatever the future holds.

Left: There's no escape from reality – an office-from-home is likely to become part of many homes, but it can be integrated comfortably into a living space.

Right: Fossil-like forms, cast in concrete, intertwine to create the base for a glass tabletop. A glass vase reveals air bubbles apparently streaming from a living plant.

glacial style

EXPLORING THE FUTURE

see it through

We have been telling each other for years that the world is shrinking. Through food, music, architecture and textiles, we have grown familiar with countries as diverse as India, Mexico and China, often without even visiting them. Television and computer technology can tell us instantly all we want to know. As mankind pushes further and further in pursuit of space and stimulation, the landscapes that will inspire advanced thinking in design are the last places we have yet to explore – the sparsely populated ice fields and glaciers.

Two factors come into play. The first is the continual drive for space in our overcrowded cities and hectic lives; the second is the technological development that has produced versatile and exciting modern materials. These twin strands are converging in a concept that will shape interior design for the next ten years – transparency.

Glass is currently one of the strongest directions in design and its appeal is easily explained. It embodies the notion of transparency, of a structure that does not block light, that can be seen through and that allows a view to whatever lies beyond it. This idea fulfils the need for emptiness and freedom, and is at the heart of this trend. Twenty-first-century living

Above: Perspex, a design material of the near future, has huge versatility, appearing as simple items such as a bowl, or even as complex structures such as a suspended floor.

Right: A simple picture created from the turquoise wool wrapped around a frame embodies a quality of insubstantiality and yet has depth, colour and texture.

involves so much time indoors, isolated from nature and reality, that we yearn for a glimpse outdoors and a reminder of the bigger picture. Larger windows and panoramic views become desirable, giving more natural daylight and less division between the inside and outside worlds.

Glass is becoming more and more widely used in commercial spheres, such as public transport, health clubs and entertainment venues. Glass technology has progressed and the possibilities are expanding and becoming more affordable. Projects that were out of the question five years ago are now achievable, so architects and designers are increasingly exploiting the unique capacities of this material. The presence of glass in buildings is becoming more familiar to the general public and the look is now filtering on to the high street and into the home.

HIDDEN WORLD

Transparency lets you see the structure or mechanism of objects. Semi-opaque computers are already with us and see-through kitchen gadgets are not far away. A glass-topped table seems more inviting than a heavy wooden or metal one. The table itself appears to take up less space than a solid piece of furniture. Glass is at once the key component and the least obvious. The fact that you can see through it, to admire the intricate construction and polished surface of the framework, and then the floor below, is all-important.

Glass gravel is the next accessory for florists and gardeners. In a clear pot or vase, this will replace conventional soil so that roots, the workings of plants, which are normally concealed below ground, are on view, reminding us of their organic origins. On another scale, a modern, glass-fronted building works in the same way. The skeleton structure and what is inside, including people, are the focus of attention, but only because of the transparency of the walls.

FANTASTIC PLASTIC

Alongside glass, other translucent man-made substances are also enjoying a revival. Plastics and Perspex are right back in fashion. We are drawn to their transparency because it gives us that vital glimpse through one object to the next. These materials are now appearing in substantial items, such as chairs and tables, and will soon replace traditional metals to produce see-through appliances, such as kettles, toasters and even fridges. Opaque Perspex flooring, lit from below by fluorescent tubes, can give the same

Right: Transparency is the major trend currently happening in garden design. A glass pot and exposed roots will transform even the most ordinary houseplant.

Below: The slimness of the furniture legs and the translucent materials almost give an impression of there being nothing there at all. The flowers appear to float in their glass vases above the table top.

see-through effect. Although you cannot actually see beneath the top surface, you have an impression of further depth, with no boundary.

SEE AND BE SEEN

Often we are unaware of evolving tastes. We just accept that one style seems preferable to another without realizing the reasons why. Like any major trend, the inclination towards translucence is not limited just to building materials and hard surfaces. It has infiltrated other aspects of how we live and the items we use. In clothing and textiles, for example, sheer fabrics are everywhere. Knitting and weaving patterns are becoming more open, with meshes, and even slashes and holes, being used for decoration with a three-dimensional aspect, replacing multi-coloured printing on to flat fabric. In the home, we are even seeing pretty ornamental nets of tiny

lights, which can be suspended to form a screen – hardly noticeable, yet delineating separate areas.

Traditional heavy curtains, which used to shut daylight out and people in, have given way to sheer floaty voiles. These maintain partial privacy but allow you to see out and also to be seen. Looking in from a distance is part of the intention and people are growing less concerned about privacy – being seen in their homes from outside.

THE HOLE STORY

The quest for substances through which light can travel has also sparked a surge in the use of perforation as a means of achieving an impression of semi-opacity in dense materials. Metal mesh is appearing in areas such as kitchen units, adding texture and interest. A humble washing-machine drum, lit from within, makes a

stunning and unconventional lamp. Minute shards of light beam out from the depths of a seemingly solid steel cylinder. Wire mesh furniture, last seen in the 1970s, is coming back with a vengeance, and semi-transparent plastic chairs with gaps in the back and arms are the newest styles. We are also witnessing the arrival of ceramic items, such as vases, with a hole integral to their shape. The search for something substantial yet not solid, beyond which we can see another space, is satisfied by these ideas.

As the environment becomes busier and more cramped, it is our natural instinct to seek out light and clarity. Human ingenuity is responsible for a polluted and overcrowded planet, but, also in part, the means to alleviate it. This means that, we can face the future with optimism, look beyond our immediate horizons – look forward.

Left: The translucence of the tabletop, chairs and floor reveals the intricate formations of the structures that support them.

Right: The aqua colours, with their associations with water, embody the glacial trend. Glass, in a variety of thicknesses, takes on the aqua tones and is a key material.

Overleaf: Light has possibilities beyond that of enabling us to see objects. Here, tiny lamps designate the desk area within the room and beams below the floor reveal its intricate structure for us to admire.

GLACIAL IDENTITY

Styles and trends are often encapsulated in a colour story. Transparency is, to an extent, the antithesis of colour, but the glacial trend has brought its own spectrum to the fore. All tones of pale blue, turquoise, lilac, aqua and green are vital to a fresh, modern interior, to the extent that they are beginning to replace traditional neutrals, such as cream and beige. They are the ideal backdrop for glassy, sandblasted and rubbed surfaces, and have their roots in frozen seas and Arctic skies.

- Glass and plastics are now the key components for transparent items, which range from vases and kettles to fridges and computers.
- Opaque materials, pierced and cut, allow natural and artificial light to shine through.
- Colours inspired by glacial scenery include pale blues and all related tones.
- Large windows and sheer curtains allow for views both inside and outside the home.

Acknowledgements

Television often gives the impression that design projects are done single-handed and with extreme ease. Nothing could be further from the truth: in fact, it takes an army of talent, skill and patience to create each design, with bagsful of help from manufacturers small and large, all pulling the stops out to make it happen on time. Mentioning each person by name here or on the listing pages is a small token of my gratitude, but it doesn't emphasize how much I appreciate and admire all these individuals and companies.

Some very special people work with me, carrying out my rough sketches and building things till they become reality – they are:
Nicola Hulme, my right-hand assistant designer and star; Weini Faloppa, my left-hand assistant designer, known as Mrs Compass; Rina Patel, assistant designer and great mimic; Wes Bolton and Frank Farci, Laurel and Hardy of the carpentry world; Robin Spilsbury, carpenter and decorator, aka Mr Tuscany; Keith Fuller, electrician, aka Mr Innuendo, and everyone else in my office.

I'm also hugely indebted to Colin Poole, photographer, who always works like a Trojan to capture all my designs, drawing energy and inspiration from the occasional feast of chocolate at 4 o'clock. Without Colin there would be no book. A big thank you also to Colin's assistants Loren Norris, Carolyn Eeles and Angie Porter. Annabelle Grundy spent hours turning my ramblings into text that made sense – what a dream to have around.

BBC TV – I would like to thank everyone who worked on the *Homefront* projects, particularly Franny Moyle, series editor. Directors – Ed Bazalgette, Ben McPherson, Paul Tucker, Katie Boyd, Helen Foulkes. Researchers – Fergus Micklejohn, Alex Steinitz, Lindi Doye, Cynthia Charles, Gordon Whistance, Tessa Carey, Alison Reynolds, Lorna Creanor and Lucyina Moodie.

Everyone at BBC Worldwide who actually put the book together, with extra special thanks to Nicky Copeland, who commissioned my proposal, the project editor Khadija Manjlai, the designer Liz Lewis and design manager Lisa Pettibone, and Pene Parker for the cover.

Mactaggart & Mickel constructed my award-winning design for the home for the future, which takes up half the book. Thanks to Bruce Mickel and Derek Mactaggart, but Ed Monaghan and Jennifer Freeman deserve extra special thanks for having to deal daily with my office, while all the workpeople below created my dream vision.

MacTaggart & Mickel staff: Jeff Duncan, Ewen Forsyth, Jennifer Freeman, David Gould, Ed Monaghan, Pauline Revels, Susan Howie. Site personnel: Alan Hunter, Jim Jamieson, Robin Gardiner, Ronnie McLeod. Joiners: Martin Anderson, Alec Chittick, Frank Duffy, David Higgins, Jamie McLean, Jim Mullighan, Steven Purdie, Lawrence Riddoch, Alec Shannon, Paul Starrit. Plumbers: Davie Smith, Frank Carbry. Labourers: Dougie Smith, Alan Carnochan, Andy Kidger, Hugh Little, Paul Martin, Rickie Martin. Bricklayers: Craig Stirling, Terry Connor, John Fraser, Don O'Holloran. Painters: Andy Gallacher, Yule Kennedy, Eddie McEnroe, Stuart McNeil, Robert Morton. Others: Andy Oliver, Wullie Gibson, Brian Gilhooly, Eric Radakovitz, Tom Kerr, George Walker, Alan Whitfield, Alec Bowie. Landscape construction: Turnbull Jeffery Partnership, Geoff and Eleanor.

Thank you all.

CREDITS

Thanks to the following organizations and individuals for supplies and services:

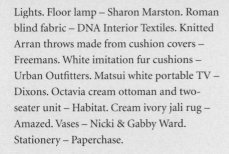

MODERN LIFESTYLE

Bamboo flooring – Mintec Corporation. Limestone and mosaic swirl flooring – Kirkstone Quarries Ltd. Caithness flagstone for fireplace – A & D Sutherland, cut by Toppolo Sterling. Fire grate – Keith Fuller Fires. Lighting track – Targetti UK. Wall pod lights – The Unnatural Light Company. Rectangular wall lights – Delta Lights. Green film on glass slits – X-Film UK Ltd. Lights hanging in front of glass slits and dining table light – Belysningsbolaget, Nielson McNally. Bendy shelves – Sarah Wakefield. Finger pots and ceramic bowls – Franny Blackburn. Tall cast ceramics – Linda Ainsworth. Perspex window covering – Ineos Acrylics, cut by QD Plastics. Blinds – Eclectics. Spiral staircase – Spiral Staircase System. Radiators – Bisque Radiators. Dining table and chairs – Octopus Modern Furniture. OXO seating – Hitch Mylius. Stereo – Empire Stores Ltd. Plugs and sockets – Clayton Munroe. Cushions – Nice Irma's. Vase – Dartington Crystal Ltd. Artwork – Karen Smith. Walnut 'S' coffee-table – Tom Schneider. White Venus light – Jon Butcher Designs. Large glass vase – Habitat.

HOME OFFICE

Bamboo flooring – Mintec Corporation. Curved glass partitions – Greenberg Glass Ltd. Roof window – Velux. Radiator – Bisque Radiators. Office furniture – Samas Roneo. Bendy shelves – Sarah Wakefield. Lights – Delta Lights. Chair – Vitra Ltd. Apple Mac computer – Bite Communications Ltd. Fax – Empire Stores Lrd. Video phone – BT. Plugs and sockets – Clayton Munroe. Artwork – Karen Smith. Ocean screen – Abigail Banyard.

THE FEEL-GOOD FACTOR

Sliding glass door – Fusion Glass Designs. Tracking for door – PC Henderson. Hot Springs radiators – Bisque Radiators. Tiles on chimney breast – Mosaik. Wall tiles – Plasterworks. White cobbles – Border Stone. Pine wooden flooring – B&Q. Imitation suede walls – JW Bollom. White upholstery pins on walls – Fisco. Ceiling light – Optelma Lights. Floor lamp – Sharon Marston. Roman blind fabric – DNA Interior Textiles. Knitted Arran throws made from cushion covers – Freemans. White imitation fur cushions – Urban Outfitters. Matsui white portable TV – Dixons. Octavia cream ottoman and two-seater unit – Habitat. Cream ivory jali rug – Amazed. Vases – Nicki & Gabby Ward. Stationery – Paperchase.

THE LIGHT STUFF

Adjustable low-voltage lights, transformers and dichroic bulbs – Christopher Wray Lighting. Timebeam projector – Aero. Flexible plywood – William T Eden. Frame – Wickes. Reinforced glass – Preedy Glass. Brackets – Homebase. Flower prints – Habitat. Rope lighting – Keith Fuller Electric. Accessories – Purves & Purves, Heal's, Nick & Gabby Ward, Elephant.

SPACE SEEKERS

Alsford Timber. Kitchen unit handles – Arthur Beale. Hob legs – Authentics. Curved island – Avon Plywood. Sink and taps – Blanco Ltd. Bin – Brabantia. Wall-mounted seating – Chris Hunsicker. Tableware – Ella Doran. Splash-back – Formica. Kitchen props – Heal's. Firedoor blank – Hitchcock & King. Dining table and chairs – IKEA. Wine rack – Jali. Builders – John Dutton & Partners. Kitchen unit carcasses – Kitchen Discount Company. Appliances – Neff. Suspended lights – Belysningsbolaget, Nielsen McNally. Glass roof – Novaglass. Worktops – Pallam Precast Ltd. Appliances – Whirlpool and Zanussi.

SLIM PICKINGS

Mini kitchen – Space Savers. Granite kitchen top – The Surrey Stone Company Ltd. Spotlights – The Light Corporation. Kitchen props – Purves & Purves. Table-top – Jali. Island table legs – Midland Chandlers. Bendy spotlights – The Light Corporation. Dining props – The Conran Shop.

THINK DIFFERENTLY

Iced glass flooring – Amtico. Ceiling lights – Targetti UK. Terrazzo worktop – Pallam Precast Ltd. Custom-made kitchen and electrical accessories – Tradestyle Cabinets. Textured glass worktops and glass partitions,

– Fusion Glass Designs Ltd. Suspension cables – Shopkit Designs Ltd. Architectural bolts – Dorma Door Controls Ltd. Caithness hob worktop and splash-back – A & D Sutherland, cut by Toppolo Sterling. Crockery and cutlery – Habitat. Pans, cooking utensils and glass containers – Muji. Drinking glasses and glass container – Habitat. Large plate – Muji. Curved breadboard – Tradestyle Cabinets. Toaster and kettle – Empire Stores Ltd. Colander, knives and salad dressing – Lakeland Ltd. Coloured ceramic bowls – Ruth Perrin. Vase – Dartington Crystal Ltd. Food props – Fratelli Sarti.

BEDROOM SPACES

Hemp rug, pale wood frames, sage green vase, prints – Habitat. Toiletries – Acca Kappa and Cologne & Cotton. Lights – IKEA. Bed linen – Dorma Bedding. Madison blankets and cushions – Melin Tregwynt. Flowers – Greens. Wood for bed head – Crispins. Castors for bed – Nu Line. Ceiling shapes – Flexi Ply. Stove – Morso. Blinds – Peter the Pleater. Chair fabric, 'Clover' from Abareque Collection – Pongees. Timber for bed – timber merchants.

RELAX WITH STYLE

Bamboo flooring – Mintec Corporation. Wall lights – Belysningsbolaget, Nielson McNally. Ceiling lights – Delta Lights. Fabric wall covering – Parker Knoll. Radiator – Bisque Radiators. Blind – Eclectics. Plugs and sockets – Clayton Munroe. Cosmetic cupboard – Carol Wilson. Bedside cubes – Habitat. Cylindrical shelves – Tom Schneider. Bed – Hitch Mylius. Eroica bed fabric – Sacho Hesslein. Throw – Anta. Satin sheets – Between the Sheets. Candles – Habitat. Free-standing light, side lights and wicker baskets – Habitat. Crystal glass vase – Dartington Crystal Ltd. Green vase – Habitat.

PRACTICAL STYLE

Sparkle flooring – Amtico. Ceiling lights – Delta Lights. Raised Prismex floor – Ineos Acrylics, made up by Stylus Graphics. Fibre-optics – Crescent Lighting. Perspex desk – Ineos Acrylics, made up by QD Plastics. Perspex chair – Bobo Designs. Television and stereo – Empire Stores Ltd. Cushions and bed cover – DNA Interior Textiles. Radiator – Bisque Radiators. Stationery – Muji and

Paperchase. Apple Mac computer – Bite Communications Ltd. E-mail phone – BT. Plugs and sockets – MK Electrical.

Second Teenage Room: Carpet tiles – Heuga. Bed, CD racks, platform, occasional beds and desk all made from MDF – timber merchants. Desk legs and platform framework – timber merchants. Rolyflex flexible plywood and desk legs – James Latham. Castors – Keystone castors. Sofa covered in charity shop jeans. Foam for occasional beds and floor cushions – Pentonville Rubber. Cushions upholstered in grey flannel – John Lewis. Cushions – Freemans. Bed linen – Dorma Bedding. Stationery – Paperchase. Cushions – The Home Place. Desk chair – Vitra.

CREATING STORAGE SPACE

Corner lights – Optelma Lighting. Taffeta walling – Pongees. Screens – Jali. Glass wardrobe doors – BLU Ltd. Wall lights – The Light Corporation. Grasses and bamboo – Greens.

THE ILLUSION OF SPACE

Floor – Amtico. Glass staircase and glass panel in floor – Armfield Glass Ltd. Consulting glass structural engineers – Alan Conisbee and Associates. Fibre-optics in glass staircase – Crescent Lighting.

FLIGHTS OF FANCY

Limestone and mosaic flooring – Kirkstone Quarries Ltd. Fibre-optic stair lights – Crescent Lighting. Ceiling lights – Targetti UK. Glass blocks – Luxcrete. Perspex – Ineos Acrylics cut by QD Plastics – Bamboo chairs – Weiming Furniture Co. Ltd. Totem screen – Salt. Artwork – Karen Smith.

Hall: Limestone and mosaic flooring – Kirkstone Quarries Ltd. Perspex – Ineos Acrylics cut by QD Plastics. Fibre-optic stair lights – Crescent Lighting. Ceiling lights – Delta Lighting Ltd. Glass blocks – Luxcrete. Console table – Octopus Modern Furniture. Vases – Dartington Crystal Ltd. Stone lights – Habitat. Wicker lights – Michael Sodeau Partnership. Wavy shelf – Tom Schneider. Candles – Habitat. Carved timber chair – Nigel Ross Sculpture.

SCULPTURAL QUALITY

Limestone and mosaic swirl flooring – Kirkstone Quarries Ltd. Lighting track – Targetti UK. Spiral staircase – Spiral Staircase System. Radiators – Bisque Radiators.

MAXIMIZE SPACE

Bathroom Towel radiator – Bisque Radiators. Japanese tub – The Mantelada Bathroom Co. Ltd. Stainless steel basin – Original Bathrooms. Toilet – Ideal Standard. Basin mixer – Ideal Standard. Ideal Response boiler – Caradon Ideal. IGO sliding glass doors – BLU Ltd. Mosaic tiles – Edgar Udny. Lights – The Light Corporation. Bathroom props – Next Directory. Toiletries – Clinique. Flooring – Amtico.

MINIMAL SOLUTION

Timber flooring – Wes Bolton & Frank Farci. Glass wall tiles – Kirkstone Quarries Ltd. Ceiling lights – Targetti UK. Stainles steel toilet, glass basin, shower rose, shower taps, basin tap, mirror and glass accessories – Original Bathrooms. Hot Springs radiator – Bisque Radiators. Perspex window coverings – Ineos Acrylics, made up by QD Plastics. Clear toilet seat – Screwy Loos. Towels – Thistletex Towels. Soaps – Lush. Shampoos, conditioners, sponges and brushes – Muji. Vase – Dartington Crystal Ltd. Canvas holder – Muji.

NO BOUNDARIES

Circular mosaic flooring – Focus Ceramics. Radiator – Bisque Radiators. Glass blocks – Luxcrete. Copper ceiling light – Concord Sylvannia. Floor lights and fibre-optics – Crescent Lighting. Mirror light – Original Bathrooms. Bath, wooden basin, toilet and shower rose – Vola Taps. Towel stand – Original Bathrooms. Perspex cover on windows – Ineos Acrylics made up by QD Plastics. Towels – Thistletex Towels. Soaps – Lush. Stone soap-dish and container – Habitat. Shampoo and bathsalts – Muji. Vase – Dartington Crystal Ltd. Blue Cathald Light – Tec Design Associates.

MILLENNIUM KITCHEN

Bamboo flooring – Mintec Corporation. Rubber flooring – Freudenberg Building Systems. Glass gravel – High Spec Gravel Ltd. Glass in floor and curved glass units – Armfield Glass Ltd. Lighting – Targetti UK. Aluminium mesh – Gooding Aluminium. Stone – Stone Age Ltd. Moving cupboards – Rackline Systems Storage Ltd. Electronics – Philips Consumer Electronics. Kitchen taps – Franke. Appliance – Zanussi. Perspex – Ineos Acrylics. Kitchenware – Brabantia. Fridge door handles – Valli & Valli Ltd. Wooden sinks – Mike Scott.

ORGANIC LIVING AND GLACIAL STYLE

Vertical totem blinds – Salt. Drum table and stool – Jam/Whirlpool. iMac computer – Apple. Cordless desktop computer – Logitech. Console table – Geoffrey Drayton. Ceramic light – Nelson. Clear acrylic nest of tables – Wood Bros Ltd. Bluebelle chair by Ross Lovegrove – Viaduct Furniture. Dining table and Fantastic Plastic Elastic Chairs – Geoffrey Drayton. Light stool – Bill Cameron. Crystaleis glass gravel – Windmill Aggregates. Neat light and mushroom chair – Habitat. Tectan floor covering – EVD (imported by Homefront; contact Tetrapak UK). Papamat rug – Crucial Trading. Coffee-table – JC Designs. Azumi chair – Ineos Acrylics. Hat stand – El Ultimo Grito. Vases – Nick & Gabby Ward. Clear Perspex – Opal ICI Perspex cut by Ineos Acrylics. Screen – Salt. Translucent zip – Iomega. Palm 5 drive portable notebook – Toshiba. Philips Micro hi-fi system. Telephone – BT. Perspex bowl – Procter-Rihl. Black chair – Dialogia. Free-standing lamp – Nelson. Plants – The Chelsea Gardener. Palms – The Palm Centre. Cobbles – Ruxley Manor Garden Centre Ltd. Transparent chair – Purves & Purves. Ceiling hazel twigs – florists. Bamboo – Jungle Giants. Ceramic pots and glasses – Habitat.

Rooms illustrated on pages 12, 14, 16, 19, 21 and 22 are from the Good Homes Show House (1998, photographer: Robin Matthews).

Suppliers

Acca Kappa
Tel: 0207 372 4101

Aero
Unit 8
Glenville Mews
Kimber Road
London
SW18 4NJ
Tel: 0208 971 0022

Linda Ainsworth
11 Johns Close
Peacehaven
East Sussex
BN10 7UQ
Tel: 01273 582670

Alsford Timber
14 Sheen Lane
London
SW14 8LW
Tel: 0208 876 2257

Amazed
Tanfield House
Wighill
Near York
LS24 8BQ
Tel: 01937 832813

Amtico Ltd
PO Box 42
Kingfield Road
Coventry
West Midlands
CV6 5PL
Tel: 0800 667766

Anta Scotland
Fearn , Tain
Ross-shire
IV20 1XW
Tel: 01862 832477

Apple Computers
Tel: 0208 218 1000

Armfield Glass Ltd
191 Church Road
Benfleet
Essex
SS7 4PN
Tel: 01268 793067

Authentics
20 High Street
Weybridge
Surrey
KT13 8AB
Tel: 01932 859800

Avon Plywood
Pixash Works
Pixash Lane
Keynsham
Bristol
BS31 1TP
Tel: 01179 861383

B&Q
Tel: 0208 466 4166
for branches

Abigail Banyard
29a Effra Road
London
SW2 1BY
Tel: 0403 229833

Barnaby
14d Wray Crescent
London
N4 3LP
Tel: 0207 281 8941

Arthur Beale
194 Shaftsbury
Avenue
London
WC2H 8JP
Tel: 0207 836 1383

**Belysningsbolaget,
Nielsen McNally**
6 Eggars Hill
Aldershot
Hampshire
GU11 3NQ
Tel: 01252 326416

**Between the
Sheets**
18 Calne Business
Centre
Harris Road
Calne
Wiltshire
SN11 9PT
Tel: 01249 821517

Bisque Radiators
15 Kingsmead
Square
Bath
BA1 2AE
Tel: 01225 469244

**Bite
Communications
Ltd**
5 Albion Court
Galena Road
London
W6 1QT
Tel: 0208 600 6719

Franny Blackburn
57 Toronto Terrace
Brighton
BN2 2UW
Tel: 01273 695114/
01494 873564

Blanco Ltd
Oxgate Lane
Cricklewood
London
NW2 7JN
Tel: 0208 452 3399

BLU Ltd
The Barn
Pilmore Lane
Watchfield
Somerset
TA9 4LB
Tel: 01278 793644

Bobo Designs
10 Southampton
Street
Brighton
East Sussex
BN2 2UT
Tel: 01273 684753

JW Bollom & Co.
PO Box 78
Croydon Road
Beckenham
Kent
BR3 4BL
Tel: 0208 658 8672

**Wes Bolton &
Frank Farci**
Tel: 07956 502067/
07956 371304

Border Stone
Buttington Quarry
Welshpool
Powys
SY21 8SZ
Tel: 01938 570253

Brabantia
Blackfriars Road
Nailse
Bristol
BS48 4SB
Tel: 01275 810600
for stockists

BT
Tel: 0800 777666

Jon Butcher
Designs
22 Paget Close
Needham Market
Ipswich
Suffolk
P6 8XF
Tel: 01449 722066

The Chelsea
Gardener
125 Sydney Street
London
SW3 6NR
Tel: 0207 352 5656

Clayton Munroe
Ltd
Kingston West
Drive
Kingston
Saverton
Totnes
Devon
Tel: 01803 762626

Clifton Nurseries
5A Clifton Villas
London
W9 2PH
Tel: 0207 286 6622

Crispins & Son
92–96 Curtain Road
London
EC2A 3AA
Tel: 0207 739 4857

Cologne & Cotton
74 Regent Street
Leamington Spa
Warwickshire
CV32 4NS
Tel: 01926 332573

Concord Sylvannia
Avis Way
New Haven
East Sussex
BN9 0ED
Tel: 01273 515811

Alan Conisbee &
Associates
(Consulting
structural engineers
– glass specialists)
1–5 Offord Street
London
N1 1DH
Tel: 0207 700 6666

The Conran Shop
Michelin House
81 Fulham Road
London
SW3 6RD
Tel: 0207 589 7401

Crescent Lighting
8 Rivermead
Pipers Lane
Thatcham
Berkshire
RG19 4EP
Tel: 01635 878888

Crucial Trading
PO Box 11
Duke Place
Kidderminster
Worcestershire
DY10 2JR
Tel: 01562 825200

Dartington Crystal
Ltd
Torrington
Devon
EX38 7AN
Tel: 01805 626262

Delta Lighting Ltd
Unit 7
Kings Road
Industrial Estate
Haslemere
Surrey
GU27 2QH
Tel: 01428 651919

Dialogia at Jinan
Ground Floor
2 Talbot Road
London

W2 5LH
Tel: 0207 229 9006

Dixons
Tel: 08000 682868

DNA Interior
Textiles
Third Floor
58 Fox Street
Glasgow
G1 4AU
Tel: 0141 248 6274

Dorma Bedding
PO Box 7
Lees Street
Swinton
Manchester
M27 6DB
Tel: 0161 251 4400

Dorma Door
Controls Ltd
Dorma Trading
Park
Staffa Road
London
E10 7QX
Tel: 0208 558 8411

Ella Doran
Unit H
Ground Floor South
95–97 Redchurch
Street
London
E2 7DJ
Tel: 0207 613 0782

Geoffrey Drayton
104 High Street
Epping
Essex
CM16 4AF
Tel: 01992 573929

John Dutton &
Partners
The Grove
London
W5 5LH
Tel: 0208 579 2723

Eclectics
Unit 25
Leigh Road
Haine Industrial
Estate
Ramsgate
Kent
CT12 5EU
Tel: 01843 852888

Elephant
230 Tottenham
Court Road
London
W1P 9AE
Tel: 0207 637 7930

El Ultimo Grito
26 Northfield
House
Frensham Street
London
SE15 6TL
Tel: 0207 732 6614

Empire Stores Ltd
18 Canal Road
Bradford
West Yorkshire
BD99 4XB
Tel: 0800 220230

EVD Tetrapac
Tel: 01978 661234/
01925 666000

Focus Ceramics
Unit 4
Hamm Moor Lane
Weybridge Trading
Estate

Weybridge
Surrey
KT15 2SF
Tel: 01932 854881

Formica
Coast Road
North Shields
Tyne & Wear
NE29 8RE
Tel: 0191 259 3000

Franke
East Park
Manchester
International Office
Centre
Styal Road
Manchester
M22 5WB
Tel: 0161 436 6280

**Freudenberg
Building Systems**
Glimorten Road
Lutterworth
Leicestershire
LE17 4DU
Tel: 01455 553081

Keith Fuller Fires
68 Clarkes Avenue
Worcester Park
Surrey
KT4 8PZ
Tel: 0208 330 0620

**Fusion Glass
Designs Ltd**
365 Clapham Road
London
SW9 9BT
Tel: 0207 738 5888

**Gooding
Aluminium**
1 British Wharf

Landmann Way
London
SE14 5RS
Tel: 0208 692 2255

**Greenberg Glass
Ltd**
Ward Park South
Industrial Estate
Cumbernauld
Strathclyde
G67 3HA
Tel: 01236 456611

Greens
125 Shepherd's
Bush Road
London
W6 7LP
Tel: 0207 603 0414

Habitat UK Ltd
196 Tottenham
Court Road

London
W1P 9LD
Tel: 0207 255 2545
(Store info line:
0645 334433)

Heal's
196 Tottenham
Court Road
London
W1P 9LD
Tel: 0207 636 1666

Heuga
Ashlyns Hall
Chesham Road
Berkhamsted
Herts
HP4 2ST
Tel: 0990 304030 for
stockists

PC Henderson
Durham Road

Bowburn
Co. Durham
DH6 5BR
Tel: 0191 377 0701

Sacho Hesslein
G24 Chelsea
Harbour Design
Centre
Chelsea Harbour
London
SW10 0XE
Tel: 0207 352 6168

**High Spec
Gravel Ltd**
Ashfield Farm
Great Confield
Essex
CM6 1LD
Tel: 01371 874115

Elizabeth Hirons
215 Oldhall Lane
Fallowhead
Manchester
M14 6HJ
Tel: 0161 834 1136

Homebase
Beddington House
Wallington
Surrey
SM6 0HB
Tel: 0645 801800 for
branches

The Home Place
The Hyde
Edgware Road
London
NW9 7TH
Tel: 0208 200 5588

House
PO Box 1748
Salisbury
Wiltshire
SP5 5SP
Tel: 01725 552549

Chris Hunsicker
7 Melton Hall

Dover Street, Ryde
Isle of Wight
PO33 2BN
Tel: 01983 811454

Ideal Standard
The Bathroom
Works
National Avenue
Hull
East Yorkshire
HU5 4HS
Tel: 01482 346461

IKEA
Brent Park
2 Drury Way
North Circular
Road
London
NW10 0TH
Tel: 0208 208 5600

Ineos Acrylics
PO Box 34
Duckworth Street
Darwen
Lancashire
BB3 1QB
Tel: 01254 874444

iomega
Tel: 0800 973194

Jali
Apsley House
Chartham
Canterbury
Kent
CT4 7HT
Tel: 01227 831710

Jam
Top Floor
1 Goodsway
London
NW1 1UR
Tel: 0207 278 5567

JC Designs
21 Park Road
Winslow, Bucks
MK18 3DL

Jungle Giants
Burford House
Gardens
10 Tenbury Wells
Worcester
WR15 8HQ
Tel: 01584 819885

**Kirkstone Quarries
Ltd**
Skelwith Bridge
Near Ambleside
Cumbria
LA22 9NN
Tel: 01539 433296

**Kitchen Discount
Company**
Unit 18
Liddell Road
Industrial Estate
Off May Grove
Road
London
NW6 2EW
Tel: 0207 372 6500

Lakeland Ltd
Alexandra Buildings
Windermere
Cumbria
LA23 1BQ
Tel: 01539 488100

John Lewis
278–306 Oxford
Street
London
W1M 9HJ
Tel: 0207 629 7711
for branches

**The Light
Corporation**
Unit 21B1
Bourne End Mills
Bourne End Lane
Hemel Hempstead
Hertfordshire
HP1 2RN
Tel: 01442 877400

Logitech
Moulin du Choc
CH-1122
Romanel sur
Morges
Switzerland
Tel: 0208 308 6582

Lush
Unit 7 and
Unit 11
The Piazza
London
WT2 8RB
Tel: 0207 240 4570

Luxcrete
Premier House
Disraeli Road
London
NW10 7BT
Tel: 0208 965 7292

**The Mantelada
Bathroom Co. Ltd**
Church View
Industrial Estate
Brompton
Northallerton
North Yorkshire
DL6 2UP
Tel: 01609 760100

Sharon Marston
Studio 54
1 Clink Street
Soho Wharf
London
SE1 9DG
Tel: 0207 234 0832

Midland Chandlers
Junction Wharf
London Road
Braunston
Daventry
North Hants
NN11 7HD
Tel: 01788 891401

Mike Scott
Tan-Yr-Efail
Llanddeusant

Anglesey
LL65 4AD
Tel: 01407 730680

**Mintec
Corporation**
17 Evelyn Gardens
London
SW7 3BE
Tel: 0207 835 1192

MK Electrical
The Arnold Centre
Paycocke Road
Basildon
Essex
SS14 3EA
Tel: 01268 563000

Morso UK Ltd
4 Wych Wood
Court
Cotswold Business
Village
London Road
Moreton-in-
Marsh
Gloucestershire

GL56 0JQ
Tel: 01608 652233

Mosaik
10 Kensington
Square
London
W8 5EP
Tel: 0207 795 6253

Muji
187 Oxford Street
London
W1R 1AJ
Tel: 0207 437 7503

Hitch Mylius
Alma House
301 Alma Rd
Enfield
Middlesex
EN3 7BB
Tel: 0208 443 2616

Neff
Grand Union
House
Old Wolverton Road

Wolverton
Milton Keynes
Bucks
MK12 5TP
Tel: 01908 328300
for stockists

Nelson
PO Box 17357
London
SW9 0WB
Tel: 0208 519 8694

Next Directory
Desford Road
Enderby
Leicester
LE9 5AT
Tel: 0345 400444

Nice Irma's
Unit 2
879 High Road
London
N12 8QD
Tel: 0208 343 7610

Noble Russell
Station Road
Uppingham
Leicestershire
LE15 9TX
Tel: 01572 821591

**Northern Feather
Home Furnishings
Ltd**
PO Box 1
Lockett Road
South Lancashire
Industrial Estate
Ashdon-in-
Makerfield
Wigan
Lancashire
WN4 8DG
Tel: 01942 721771

Novaglass
8 Mill Way
Old Mill Lane
Industrial Estate
Mansfield Wood
House
Nottingham

NG19 5AL
Tel: 01623 420788

Nu-Line Builders Merchants
315 Westbourne Park Road
London
W11 1EF
Tel: 0207 727 7748

Octopus Modern Furniture
51 Bowlynn
East Moorside
Sunderland
SR3 2SU
Tel: 0191 522 8629

Optelma Lighting
14 Napier Court
The Science Park
Abingdon
Oxon
OX14 4NB
Tel: 01235 553769

Original Bathrooms
143–145 Kew Road
Richmond
Surrey
TW9 2PN
Tel: 0208 940 7554

Pallam Precast Ltd
187 West End Lane
London
NW6 2LJ
Tel: 0207 328 6512

The Palm Centre
Ham Nursery
Ham Street
Richmond
Surrey
TW10 7AH
Tel: 0208 255 6191

Paperchase
213 Tottenham Court Road
London
W1P 9AF
Tel: 0207 580 8496
for branches

Parker Knoll Fabrics and Wallpapers
PO Box 30
West End Road
High Wycombe
Bucks
HP11 2QD
Tel: 01494 467411

Pentonville Rubber Company
104 Pentonville Road
London
N1 9JB
Tel: 0207 837 4582

Ruth Perrin
25 Laverstoke Lane
Laverstoke
Near Whitchurch
Hampshire
RG28 7NY
Tel: 07957 305522

Peter the Pleater
17–19 Great Eastern

Street
London
EC2A 3EN
Tel: 0207 375 1053

Phillips Consumer Electronics
Tel: 08706 010101

Plasterworks
38 Cross Street
London
N1 2BG
Tel: 0207 226 5355

Pongees
28–30 Hoxton Square
London
N1 6NN
Tel: 0207 739 9130

Preedy Glass
Lamb Works
North Road
London
N7 9DP
Tel: 0207 700 0377

Proctor-Rihl
63 Cross Street
London
N1 2BB
Tel: 0207 704 6003

Purves & Purves
Tottenham Court Road
London
W1P 9HD
Tel: 0207 580 8223

QD Plastics
1 Elm Road
Broadmeadow
Industrial Estate
Glasgow
G82 2RH
Tel: 01389 762377

Rackline Systems Storage Ltd
Oaktree Lane

Talke
Newcastle-under-Lyme
Staffordshire
ST7 1RX
Tel: 01782 777666

Nigel Ross Sculpture
East Cottage
Hillocks of Gourdie
Blair Gowrie
Perthshire
PH10 6RF
Tel: 01250 884778

Ruxley Manor Garden Centre Ltd
Maidstone Road
Sidcup
Kent
DA14 5BQ
Tel: 0208 300 0084

Salt
117 Oxo Tower Wharf
Bargerhouse Street
London
SE1 9PH
Tel: 0207 593 0007

Tom Schneider
20 Frognal Way
Hampstead
London
NW3 6XE
Tel: 0208 275 0306

Samas Roneo
10 Great Titchfield Street
London
W1T 7AA
Tel: 01332 673326

Screwy Loos
PO Box 523
Newcastle-under-Lyme
Staffordshire
ST5 2RT
Tel: 01782 719120

Shopkit Designs Ltd
100 Cecil Street
North Watford
Hertfordshire
WD2 5AP
Tel: 01923 818282

Karen Smith
49c Harwood Road
London
SW6 4QL
Tel: 0207 371 9755

Michael Sodeau Partnership
25d Highgate West Hill
London
N6 6NP
Tel: 0208 341 2026

Space Savers
222 Kentish Town Road
London
NW5 2AD
Tel: 0207 485 3266

Spiral Staircase System
Lewes Design Contracts Ltd
The Mill, Glynde
Lewes
East Sussex
BN8 6SS
Tel: 01273 858341

Stone Age Ltd
19 Filmer Road
London
SW6 7BU
Tel: 0207 385 7954

Stylus Graphics
Unit 3
Listerhills Science Park
Campus Road
Bradford
West Yorkshire
BD7 1HR
Tel: 01274 736191

**Surrey Stone
Company Ltd**
Pew Corner
Artington Manor
Farm
Old Portsmouth
Road
Artington, Guildford
Surrey
GU3 1LP
Tel: 01483 300109

A & D Sutherland
Spittal Quarry
Caithness
KW1 5XR
Tel: 01847 84123

Targetti UK
6 Stanton Gate
Mawney Road
Romford, Essex
RM7 6HL
Tel: 01708 741286

Phil Taylor
22 Stewart Close
Spondon
Derby
DE21 7FB
Tel: 01332 673326

**The Unnatural
Light Company**
6 Mentmore
Terrace
London
E8 3PN
Tel: 0208 986 5139

Thistletex Towels
38 Watt Road
Hillington
Glasgow
G52 4RW
Tel: 0141 882 4455

Toffolo Sterling
Wallace House
White House Road
Stirling
FK7 7TA
Tel: 01786 450560

Tradestyle Cabinets
7 Glentanar Road
Balmore Industrial
Estate
Glasgow
G22 7XS
Tel: 0141 336 3623

Melin Tregwynt
Melin Tregwynt
Mill
Castlemorris
Haverfordwest
Pembs
SA62 5UX
Tel: 01348 891 694

**Turnbull Jeffery
Partnership**
Sandeman House
Edinburgh
EH1 1SR
Tel: 0131 557 5050

Edgar Udny & Co
314 Balham High
Road
London
SW17 7AA
Tel: 0208 767 8181

Urban Outfitters
36–38 Kensington
High Street
London
W8 4PF
Tel: 0207 761 1001

**The Velux
Company Ltd**
Woodside Way
Glenroches
East Fife
KY7 4ND
Tel: 01592 772211

Viaduct Furniture
1–10 Summers
Street
London
EC1R 5BD
Tel: 0207 278 8456

Valli & Valli Ltd
8 Gerard Road
Lichfield Road
Industrial Estate
Tamworth
Staffordshire
B79 7UW
Tel: 01827 63352

Vitra Ltd
121 Milton Park
Abingdon
Oxon
OX14 4SA
Tel: 01235 820400
for stockists

Vola Taps
Unit 12
Ampthill Business
Park
Station Road
Bedfordshire
MK45 2QW
Tel: 01525 841155

Sarah Wakefield
85 Watersite Place
Sheering Lower
Road
Sawbridgeworth
Herts
CM21 9RF
Tel: 01279 600875

Wood Bros Ltd
Marsh Lane
London Road
Ware
Hertfordshire
SG12 9QH
Tel: 01920 469241
for stockists

**Weiming Furniture
Co. Ltd**
Suite One
62 Bell Road
Sittingbourne
Kent
ME10 4HE
Tel: 01795 472262

Whirlpool
PO Box 45
209 Purley Way
Croydon
Surrey
CR9 4RY
Tel: 0208 649 5013

**Wickes Building
Supplies Ltd**
Station Road
Harrow
Middlesex
HA1 2QB
Tel: 0500 300328

Carol Wilson
1 Stanthorpe Road
London
SW16 2ED
Tel: 0208 6778208

**Windmill
Aggregates**
Windmill Works
Aythorpe Roding
Great Dunmow

Essex
Tel: 01279 876987

**Christopher Wray
Lighting**
591 Kings Road
London
SW6 2YW
Tel: 0207 736 8434

X-Film UK Ltd
PO Box 37
34 Bilton Way
Luton
Bedfordshire
LU1 1XB
Tel: 01582 453308

Zanussi
PO Box 530
55–57 High Street
Slough
Berkshire
SL1 1BE
Tel: 0990 140140

Index

Page references in *italic* refer to illustrations, those in **bold** refer to room plans